LONDON HOMES

Burlington House, showing the eighteen-century Forecourt as it existed a hundred years ago. The Mansion is incorporated in the present building

LONDON HOMES

By
RALPH DUTTON

SALVE REGINA
COLLEGE LIBRARY

LONDON
ALLAN WINGATE
12 BEAUCHAMP PLACE S.W.3

First published in 1952 by
ALLAN WINGATE (PUBLISHERS) LTD.
12 Beauchamp Place, London S.W.3

/

Made and printed in Great Britain by
William Clowes and Sons, Limited, London and Beccles

PRINTED IN GREAT BRITAIN

Contents

▼

Acknowledgment

The illustrations of the Bayswater Road, facing page 20, of Soho Square, facing page 58, and of Dorchester House, facing page 114, are reproduced by kind permission of the Director and Secretary of the Victoria and Albert Museum; and that of Bedford House and Bloomsbury Square, facing page 39, by kind permission of His Grace the Duke of Bedford. Those facing pages 100 and 115, and on page 124, are from the Author's collection. The remainder are reproduced from originals in the *Picture Post* Library.

List of Illustrations

I

Restoration London

The return of the Stuart dynasty to the throne of England marked the opening of a great epoch of artistic development in this country. It was an epoch covering a little more than a century and a half and was to see the growth and blossoming of the decorative arts, followed by their melancholy decline after the first quarter of the nineteenth century to the standards exemplified at the Great Exhibition of 1851. The age began under the most propitious auspices. There was a sense of spring in the air: the dark days of the Commonwealth, which had in fact provided benefits for many, were thrust into the past, and the common people, who stood to gain very little, acclaimed their monarch with the utmost enthusiasm. Voltaire, who had spoken with men who were present, describes how a crowd of twenty thousand men and women, many in tears, fell on their knees as the tall, cadaverous young man stepped on to English soil. These scenes of popular hysteria were repeated and even excelled when, shortly afterwards, he entered London, passing beneath the flamboyant arches and decorations contrived in his honour by that versatile and scheming character Sir Balthazar Gerbier. The people were in no doubt about the prosperity and pleasure they anticipated from the return of the monarchy, but the King on his side must have viewed with the utmost misgiving the strong Presbyterian tone he found in the members of the Parliament which had voted for his restoration. Perhaps with a foreboding of future events, the first laws to be passed by the Commons were aimed at curtailing the very entertainments and vices which were to be an outstanding feature of Charles's reign. Such amusements as masques, bear-baiting and dancing round maypoles, which had in some degree survived Cromwellian austerity, were declared illegal; while adultery, always a popular pastime, was to be punishable by death. The naked human form was no longer to appear either in sculpture or painting, and where this shocking spectacle already existed it was at once to be modified by the introduction of suitably placed drapery or foliage.

Here was to be seen an attitude of mind which provided little comfort or hope for those who expected to practise or to benefit by the arts under the genial sunshine of the monarchy. But fortunately this rigid attitude was not one which long endured, and within a year or two the Court and in a large measure the people had passed happily into the manners and modes which we associate with the later Stuart age. At the same time the decorative arts prospered, and of these none more so than architecture, in which the English were to equal, if they did not excel, their brilliant Continental rivals. The impulse to build, and usually to over-build, has always been an amiable characteristic of the English; and after a period of restriction, such as the majority of the rich had suffered during the Civil Wars and Commonwealth, the urge seems to have reached uncontrollable force. A large part of this energy was devoted to the alteration, enlargement or construction of country houses, but in London also, and in its immediate neighbour-hood, there was an immense expansion in building of houses on all scales. The Restoration, therefore, seems a suitable point from which to set out on a tour of the vanished and also still existing houses of London.

Although the years following the Restoration were, generally speak-ing, an age of widespread construction, they were, preceded, in so far as the City of London was concerned, by a period of intense destruction. The term was short, only four days, but this sufficed for the Great Fire to sweep over an area of four hundred and thirty-six acres and con-sume the production of centuries of domestic and ecclesiastical building. The devastation, except on the west, was confined within the ancient walls of the City, which extended in a wide semi-circle from the Fleet river flowing at the foot of Ludgate Hill to the moats and fortifications of the Tower of London on the east. To the north the wall separated the town from the open lands of Moor Fields, while on the south the city was bounded by the gently curving banks of the great waterway, which had led to the foundation of a settlement on this site. A century and a half before the Restoration the city was still restricted within its walls, and there was little extra-mural building except for isolated houses in particularly favoured places, such as on the river bank. The town fast became unduly congested and methods of checking this unwelcome growth were a constant preoccupation of the Crown and the City authorities. The recurring outbreaks of plague produced an occasional and temporary alleviation; but pestilence, like war, forms no permanent hindrance to a growing population, and overcrowding was soon as serious as ever. Some relief was achieved by the Dissolution of the Monasteries. There were no fewer than twenty-three cloisters situated in the City and immediately across the river on the south

2

bank: all had large and spreading buildings, many owned spacious gardens and orchards. When the orders were disbanded the conventual buildings were usually handed over to the king's deserving friends for conversion to domestic purposes, and houses were constructed in part of the gardens. The churches were occasionally allowed to survive to form the ecclesiastical centre of a parish. The church of St. Bartholomew the Great is an example of one of these rare reprieves, though only the massive Norman choir of Rahere's priory church was left standing. The space thus provided by the king's rapacity proved, however, to be no more than a temporary panacea to the recurring problem of over-population, and indeed eventually added to the difficulty of the situation, since, with so many men and women released from their condition of celibacy, the birth-rate mounted with ever-increasing speed.

Before the death of Queen Elizabeth the City had burst the bounds formed by the ancient walls, and buildings were beginning to cover the meadows which encircled the ramparts on the west side from the river-bank to Moor Fields. At the time of the Restoration building had both thickened and spread still farther west towards the royal domain at Whitehall; while along the Strand there was "continuall new building of divers fair houses", according to Stow's *Survey of London*, which was begun in 1598, enlarged in 1618 and re-issued in 1633. The general appearance of the City, before the Great Fire caused such radical change, may be seen in the engravings of Hollar made in the middle of the seventeenth century. They were an early parallel to the aerial photograph of the present day, and form a single panorama of the stretch of river from Westminster to the Tower. The viewpoint is sited at various spots in the air about five hundred feet above the meadows and buildings on the south bank, and so affords a prospect of the whole of the northern shore with the great houses fronting the water, the crowded buildings behind and the rolling open country beginning within a short distance of the centre of the town. On the western extremity there rises the clumsy outline of the unfinished building of Westminster Abbey, then without the twin towers which were to be added in the following century, while a short way to the east, beyond the jumble of towers and courts which formed Whitehall Palace, stands the solid structure of Inigo Jones' Banqueting House. A strange interloper it appears with its serene façades of great height and the horizontal emphasis of its cornices and mouldings contrasting sharply with the gables, mullioned windows and tall chimney-stacks

3

of the houses which surround it. The majority of the large houses which lay between Whitehall and the City were set close to the Strand, which formed their approach from the land side, while their gardens extended down to the level of high water, and thence stairs descended for the convenience of those arriving by boat. A few, such as the Savoy, stood close to the bank, while the medieval towers and walls of Baynards Castle rose direct from the water like a fortified building from a moat. Farther east as the Thames flowed past the City the buildings crowded to the water's edge; some were raised on arcades and others presented bastion walls pierced by water-gates against the perils of floods and spring tides. Behind these buildings on the rise of Ludgate Hill stood the long Gothic form of St. Paul's Cathedral, solid yet graceful and showing no indication of the weakness which was assailing its structure at the time that Hollar was composing his panorama.

The buildings in the middle distance are carefully drawn, but even more clearly defined are the layout and structures which Hollar found in the foreground as he assumed his aerial sketching stool. The space bounded by the wide curve of the river opposite Whitehall and the fine houses of the Strand, now dominated by Waterloo Station, was completely pastoral with a few cottages embowered in trees and cattle grazing in the meadows. Farther east at Southwark, where London Bridge, surmounted by a fabulous construction of gateways, houses and shops, formed the only permanent link between the City and the south bank, there was a little town of jostling houses set amidst the encircling meadows. The spreading Tudor structure of Winchester House, long deserted by the bishops of that see but still surrounded by an admirable garden with a circular pool and fountain and several enclosures of orchard, lay to the west of the bridge; while round its walls were narrow streets of closely packed Tudor and Elizabethan houses. These were not the homes of the rich, but were the little three-storied houses with timbered gables and small lattice windows of the working classes. Many had narrow yards behind them, but nothing which could be looked on as a garden, although space was not particularly precious with open meadows so near at hand.

Two very similar circular buildings stand out in the panorama, one is labelled "Globe" the other "Beere Bayting". The former was not the wooden building in which Shakespeare had acted, for this had been burnt in 1613, but in its circular form, "this wooden O", it must have conformed to the shape of the original. The second rotunda was devoted to the sport which the Parliament of the Restoration made gallant but unavailing efforts to suppress. Bear-baiting must have been a tedious entertainment, but it was one which had been as popular with the Court as with the lower classes. Stow gives an account of a very lavish display, a gala performance apparently, which was put on to celebrate the creation of King James I's eldest son, Henry, as Prince of Wales in 1610. The first entrant to the arena was a bear of unusual size and ferocity, which had lately killed a child "negligently left in the bear-house", the blame for the catastrophe attaching rather to the bear than to the parents. The grill of the lion's den was next opened and a terrifying animal emerged, but disappointingly paid no attention to the bear; two mastiffs were then introduced which, ignoring the bear, set rather half-heartedly on the lion. In order to instil a little excitement into this unspirited contest, a stallion was added to the assembled animals, but remained unconcerned until attacked by six more dogs which had been put into the ring. At last there was a little cruelty and bloodshed, but before the stallion had been worried to death, the king ordered its removal; while the lion, showing obvious signs of relief, was allowed to return to its den. Several other lions were released, but all eluded the bear's embraces and escaped into their dens as soon as the doors were opened. The bear was thus the victor amongst its animal opponents, and it fell to human beings to bait it to death in the usual savage manner. It is comforting to note that £20 of the takings from this stimulating spectacle were handed to the bereaved parents.

Above the throng of gabled roofs and twisted chimneys on the north bank rose, like plants seeking the light, the robust Gothic towers of the City churches, their solid forms, relieved by occasional finials and battlements, blending harmoniously with the long lines and truncated tower of the great cathedral which stood amongst them. Within a few years the silhouette of the City was to be radically changed, and the low outline was to be pierced by the pillared cupolas and belfries, constructed in the gleaming silver of Portland stone, devised by Sir Christopher Wren's inexhaustible genius.

The constant preoccupation of the Crown with the problem of the growth of the thriving capital seems at this distance somewhat inexplicable; but from Henry VIII to Charles I each monarch in turn, and his advisers, accepted as a settled policy the necessity for reducing building to a minimum. Various reasons were at times advanced, such as that there would be difficulty in bringing adequate supplies of food to a town of great size and that famine might ensue; or that further building might lead to a greater likelihood of plague and other diseases breaking out and spreading, and that the danger of fire would be increased. In the event, the Crown's restrictions brought about the very calamities which it was hoped to avoid, since with an ever-increasing population and a more or less stationary amount of accommodation. the overcrowding which existed within the romantic-looking little houses, which Hollar portrayed, became appalling. The holocausts of 1665 and 1666 were the direct and final results. If it were proposed to build a new house in or near the City, before permission was granted it had first to be proved that the new building would rise on the foundations of an old and that no new ground would be covered; if a house were erected without permission it was often compulsorily demolished. The regulations, indeed, were as strict as those which exist today, though as will be seen, they were by no means always enforced and after the Restoration they were generally abandoned. The menace of fire was constantly in the minds of the authorities, and, together with the restrictions on indiscriminate building, went the firmest regulations on the materials to be employed in those houses which were allowed. The use of timber in construction was very early forbidden; in the reign of Richard I the Mayor of London had ordered that all houses should be built of stone and that party walls must be of considerable thickness. If these rules had been adhered to, it would not have been necessary for James I and Charles I to issue such stringent regulations more than four centuries later. The Stuart instructions were exceedingly detailed, and covered such matters as the thickness of walls, the size of windows and doors, and the heights of rooms, which, with unexpected lavishness, were to be ten feet for the ground floor and seven and a half feet for those above; overhanging upper floors, which had been a characteristic of the vernacular style of the previous centuries, were sternly forbidden. There seems to have been no limit set to the total height of houses, and Stow remarks that there are "many houses of four or five stories". The "fair house of Sir John Champnies, Alderman and Mayor of London" in Tower Street, however, was sufficiently unusual for Stow to give it a special description: "He builded in his house a high Tower of bricke, the first that I ever heard of in any private man's house, to overlook his neighbours in the Citie." If Sir John had proposed spending an agreeable old age observing the happenings in the gardens of his neighbours, he was disappointed, for he lost his sight some years before his death and so was unable to put his lookout point to the advantage he had anticipated.

The River Front and the Tower before the Great Fire. From Visscher's
view of 1616

The Great Fire of London, 1666

A Bishop's Mansion on the South Bank : Winchester House in 1647

An eighteenth-century view of the North Bank at the "Waterhouse",
looking to Westminster Bridge

An additional reason for official attempts to keep London to a moderate size may have been anxiety about the water supply, which early in the seventeenth century was becoming inadequate to the increasing demands. Stow mentions that in a number of wards there was a "fair-water conduit of Thames water". There was one in Bishopsgate and another in Downegate, "castellated, and made in the year 1568". The latter must have been of large size, since in 1574, when it was unusually full after a violent storm, a lad of eighteen fell into it and was drowned in spite of efforts to rescue him. In one of Hollar's views there can be seen a tall building, shaped like an obelisk, rising from the banks of the Thames close to the water's edge between the "stairs" of Arundel and Somerset Houses, which is labelled "Waterhouse". This building contained one of the "water-engines" which Chamberlayne mentions in his *Present State of England* as providing "excellent wholesome water" pumped from the Thames. It stood until the end of the eighteenth century and appears, an unmistakable structure with its long perpendicular lines, in the pictures of Samuel Scott, Thomas Malton and other portrayers of London's waterfront. Chamberlayne's work was completed twenty-seven years after the Restoration, but the Thames still formed the principal supply though its water, in spite of the author's eulogies, must have been dangerously polluted. There were other supplies of purer water available, but they were strangely neglected. The Conduit Fields on the rising ground to the north of London contained springs which were utilized to a limited extent, and Stow describes a "Great Conduit of sweet water conveyed by pipes of lead underground from Paddington". This supply had been enlarged in 1479, but the quantity of water was still small when Stow was writing in the seventeenth century. Ever since 1613, however, while the inhabitants of London were content to make use of the contaminated water flowing past their walls or of the piddling provision from Paddington, there existed, barely a mile distant from the City at Islington, a supply both pure and fully adequate to the needs of the town.

The making of the New River was one of the greatest engineering feats of the early seventeenth century. The project had long been considered, but it was not until 1606 that the Corporation had been authorized by act of parliament to bring a water supply from the magnificent springs at Chadwell and Amwell, near Ware in Hertfordshire, to the northern outskirts of London. It had been ascertained that the proposal was feasible in that there was sufficient fall in levels

7

for water to run between the two points; but no one had the enter-prise to undertake the work until 1609, when Hugh Myddleton, a friend of Sir Walter Raleigh and a member of Parliament, offered to carry out the scheme. On April 1st, 1609, work was begun, and by Michaelmas Day 1613 a channel ten feet wide by four feet deep and following a meandering course of almost forty miles through the meadows of Hertfordshire and Middlesex, discharged the first water into reservoirs at Islington amidst a scene of great public jubilation and enthusiasm. The difficulties had proved even greater than had been anticipated, and if the king had not given financial assistance the work could hardly have been completed. The whole of Myddleton's fortune was sunk in the company and it was not until long after his death in 1631 that it became a highly remunerative concern; meanwhile little advantage was taken of this splendid water, which had been brought to London with such difficulty and cost.

Water supply and drainage must inevitably advance together. Before the Great Fire the gutters in the streets were considered con-venient receptacles for every kind of filth, but when the City was rebuilt sewers were laid along the main streets and westwards along Fleet Street and the Strand, which carried the refuse away into the Thames. The smaller streets had still to be content with open gullies. Simultaneously domestic drainage of a sort was devised. Pipes led down through the houses to cesspits in the cellars, which when filled would be pumped out into the gutters. This arrangement was even less hygienic than no drains at all, and it is hardly surprising that Francis North, later Lord Keeper Guildford, found it intolerable in the fine new house he leased in Chancery Lane in 1675. The constant emptying of the cesspits into the gutters produced an insupportable stench, and with the last outbreak of the plague only a decade away, North decided it was essential to remedy the situation. Against great local opposition he obtained a decree ordering all householders to make drains to connect their pits with a pipe passing down the Lane, which discharged into "the grand common sewer in Fleet Street". It was a system which was gradually to become universal.

The attempts of the authorities may have checked, but it certainly failed to prevent all building. Though all were supposed to ask per-mission, it seems that it was the poor rather than the rich who received the refusals. For a century or two before the Restoration the mile and a half of road running south-westward from Ludgate in a wide curve following the bank of the river to Whitehall and Westminster had gradually become lined with fine houses for the whole of its length. The greater number of these houses, Essex, Somerset, The Savoy, Russell, Durham, York, Northumberland, Suffolk, belonging either to great territorial nobles or to the princes of the Church, lay between the roadway and the water; but a few, such as Bedford House, with its

Northumberland House, Charing Cross

spacious garden, stood on the north side. As the highway turned due south it entered the royal precincts of Whitehall and passed under the tall gateway designed by Holbein into the conglomeration of buildings which formed the palace. This was not ancient royal property, but like Hampton Court Palace, it had been secured for the Crown by

Henry VIII's astuteness in engineering the fall of Wolsey in 1529. Hampton Court was the greater prize, but York House, as Whitehall was then called, proved a useful and convenient addition to the not very lavish number of royal palaces. The see of York was recompensed with a more modest building along the river bank, and Henry entered with immense pleasure into the Cardinal's spacious house, which earned its new name from the gleaming white stone in which it was constructed. The magnificent style in which Wolsey had lived can never have been equalled by any of the subsequent royal owners. The rooms were hung with cloth of gold and silver, with tapestry and velvets; tables were loaded with plate of silver and gilt, while one cupboard contained vessels of solid gold. The Cardinal's copes were the most splendid, the most lavishly embroidered, the most richly encrusted with jewels that had ever been seen in this country. His train consisted of no less than eight hundred persons, all elaborately dressed, even the head cook wearing a satin jerkin and a chain of gold round his neck. This at least is how the way of life at York House appeared to the dazzled eyes of Wolsey's biographer, Cavendish, but it is possible that the description is as highly embroidered as the Cardinal's copes. If Shakespeare's relation of events is correct it was here, during one of Wolsey's routs, that Henry first saw Anne Boleyn; in any event it was here that their hole-and-corner marriage took place on January 25th, 1533. Capacious though Whitehall was, it was not large enough for the King; and in 1536 he added a number of "distinct, beautiful, costly and pleasant lodgings". He also enclosed a large park with a wall of brick and stone, and thus formed an area extending from the Sanctuary at Westminster almost to Charing Cross, to the whole of which was given the name of the King's Palace of Westminster.

These royal precincts, then, were first joined to the City by a single curving ribbon of great houses, but slowly the ribbon of building broadened northward. In 1570 the modest little church of St. Martin, on the rising ground above Whitehall, was still literally "in the Fields", but the meadows bordering St. Martin's Lane were being replaced by houses and gardens, and by 1660, the City and the Palace of Westminster had coalesced into a single if elongated whole. Though in plan it merged into a single unit, London remained a body with two hearts. There was what Macaulay calls "the metropolis of commerce" centred on the Exchange and "the metropolis of fashion" revolving round the Palace. In the years following the Restoration the relative importance of these two spheres remained about equal: those hoping to make fortunes by commercial means lived and laboured in the City, those who considered that royal favour was an easier means to success frequented Whitehall. The former was perhaps more solid, the latter more elegant; but undoubtedly great material benefits could be secured in both places by those sufficiently cunning. With the Great Revolution, however, the situation began to alter. It was no longer the King but his advisers who dispensed the coronets, garters and bishoprics. Thus the predatory courtiers who had thronged round Charles II moved to more rewarding pastures, and the City became the undisputed centre of London.

Both these twin hubs of metropolitan life were destroyed by fire. The first re-arose in a few years from its ashes, as is symbolized by the phoenix which surmounts Wren's tall Monument, standing close to the site of the bakery in which the fire broke out; but the rambling palace, which was destroyed in 1698, was never rebuilt. "Whitehall burnt", wrote Evelyn succinctly in his diary; "nothing but walls and ruins left." He exaggerated, however, for the Banqueting House, which stood at a distance from the main buildings survived. Thus it is still possible to assess the immense loss which the architecture of London suffered by the abandonment of the scheme for the building of a vast new palace, of which the Banqueting House formed a very small part. Wren drew up several ambitious plans for rebuilding a palace on the site of the charred debris, but William III's heart was not in the project, and the Palace of Westminster survives merely as a palace in name. Though the disaster to the City was much greater, its resurrection was swiftly achieved. Within a few months of the conflagration an "Exact Survey of the Streets, Lanes, Churches contained within the Ruins of the City of London " was published by John Leake, and this clearly shows the small area of houses which survived intact within the walls, and also the distance to which the fire penetrated to the west. The flames swept over the boundaries at the foot of Ludgate Hill, across the Fleet river, and were not extinguished until they reached Fetter Lane on the north side of Fleet Street, and a point almost up to Temple Stairs on the south. The area lying north-west of the City round Holborn was unharmed.

No sooner had the fire passed than Christopher Wren and John Evelyn were clambering over the still smoking remains, measuring, planning, calculating, so that within a very few days each had drawn up a scheme for laying out the new city on spacious and dignified lines. Wren's proposal for long, straight thoroughfares, ninety feet wide, converging on such major buildings as St. Paul's, the Guildhall and the Exchange, with a symmetrical arrangement of connecting streets and a "commodious Key" running the whole length of the river frontage, was a splendid conception and would have gone a long way to remove the traffic problems of this day. But with the area of the City in the hands of a great number of small freeholders, most of whom wished to rebuild on the original sites of their vanished homes, it proved impossible to reconstruct streets on entirely new lines as Wren envisaged. Thus the old streets and alleys kept their original entity and houses were rebuilt piecemeal without any attempt at a general effect of splendour. In general, however, conditions in the new City must have been better than in the old if Chamberlayne's adulatory description of 1687 is near the truth. "They have made their Streets much more large and streight, paved each side with smooth hewn stone . . . and whereas before they dwelt in low, dark, wooden Cottages, they now live in lofty, lightsome, uniform, Brick Buildings."

Although a disaster to almost all strata of the community, the Great Fire provided a splendid and profitable opportunity for the speculative builder. This profession, when considered in conjunction with Greater London of today, has a singularly ominous ring, but in general the Carolean builders, constructing their solid brick houses, seem, by the nature of the prevailing style of architecture, to have left little but beauty in their wake. One of the most successful followers of this risky profession was Dr. Nicholas Barbon. The doctor is thought to have been the son of Praisegod Barebones who gave his austere name to Cromwell's "Little" Parliament. The father's attempts to prevent the restoration of Charles II do not seem to have interfered with the success of the son's career. Starting in the medical profession, he was a Doctor of Medicine of Utrecht, he later turned his attention to the more rewarding business of providing houses for the homeless. He also devised a system of fire insurance, the first in this country, of which Narcissus Luttrell wrote rather coldly in his *Brief Relation* of 1681 "he is likely to gett vastly by it". Besides his work in the devastated spaces of the City, he built several fine houses in Chancery Lane, and it was most probably in one of these that Francis North installed his hygienic drainage system. In addition Barbon bought the open area of Red Lion Fields, on the north side of Holborn, where now stand the square and street of that name. The urbanization of this locality was not achieved without difficulty, for "the gentlemen of Graie's

Whitehall Palace and its Park in the reign of James II

Whitehall Palace in the eighteenth century: the Banqueting House
and Scotland Yard

Downing Street in 1827: from a drawing by J. C. Buckler

The Piazza, Covent Garden, in 1764

Inn", which adjoined the fields, objected to this encroachment and a serious riot took place between them and the workmen engaged on the site. The area of Hatton Garden on the other side of Gray's Inn was already partly built over, as can be seen in Leake's *Exact Survey*, but the houses were set far apart in large gardens and orchards, while Hatton Garden itself was an open space. Another of Barbon's enterprises, which has a modern sound, was the purchase of Essex House, one of the great houses standing between the Strand and the river bank. He demolished the building and erected small houses, tenements, and taverns on the site. It was a fate which was to come to almost every one of the great houses forming the long chain connecting the City with Whitehall; but at the time it was considered as an affront to this desirable neighbourhood, the acme of riches and elegance on one side and of sobriety and industry on the other, if indeed the latter represented a true picture of the life led in the robust brick chambers lately erected by Wren in the Temple. Moreover on the east side of the Temple buildings there already lay the deplorable area of Whitefriars.

No district could have had a more misleading name, a name so suggestive of piety and charity, of the simple, useful lives passed by the Carmelite brothers in their cloistered seclusion. Such, in fact, had been the condition for several centuries in this pleasant establishment on the banks of the Thames; but the precincts had always also been a sanctuary for wrongdoers. Although the friars had been cast out at the Reformation, the place still retained the privilege of providing protection for debtors. Thus the buildings were crowded from cellar to attic, not only with those in financial difficulties, but also with criminals and vagabonds of both sexes, who were here beyond the effective reach of the law. So dangerous were these desperate characters, so united in their resistance to any intruder, that it was impossible to execute a warrant without the protection of a company of musketeers. All night through the coarse sounds of drunken quarrelling and singing disturbed the dignified atmosphere of the Inner Temple, which lay so uncomfortably adjacent. The authorities seemed at a loss to deal with this nuisance, which all agreed was intolerable, until at last in 1697 a bill was passed abolishing the franchise both of Whitefriars and of the Savoy, which possessed similar privileges. The inhabitants were allowed a fortnight's grace, during which breathing space there was a wholesale flight overseas or to other dark corners of the town, and when the Sheriff's officers entered the squalid warren of tenements it was found to be absolutely deserted.

The darkness of the streets of London added greatly to their danger. No organized system of lighting existed, and it was not until 1684 that an enterprising contractor, named Edward Heming, obtained the exclusive right of lighting the streets for a term of years. He undertook to place a light in front of every tenth door from six to midnight on all moonless nights from Michaelmas to Lady Day; in return for this amenity he received a very moderate payment. Heming can have brought his modest illumination to no more than a small part of the town, but where it existed it added greatly to the safety of the streets. Many houses built towards the end of the seventeenth century and later were provided with their own lanterns, supported, as may still be seen, on standards of forged iron rising on either side of the steps to the main entrance, or, as at No. 10 Downing Street, on an arch of iron spanning the steps. These must have formed a useful supplement to Heming's sparse beacons.

Dr. Barbon may have been one of the first true examples of the speculative builder, but there were others who had even earlier benefited from the uncontrollable expansion of London. Of these latter Francis, 4th Earl of Bedford, was an instance, and was the first of the landowners in the immediate vicinity of the City and Whitehall to undertake the laying out of streets and the building of houses on land they were fortunate enough to possess in the area. A number were to follow his precedent in the following century. Lord Bedford was most happily placed in that his ancestor, the 1st Earl, had received at the Dissolution, amongst many other estates, the site covering seven acres lying on the north side of the Strand which had formed a garden belonging to the Abbey and Convent of Westminster. On the south side of this agreeable site Bedford House was built, facing east, with its south end abutting on to the street. "A large but old built house, having a great Yard before it, for the reception of coaches" was Strype's description of it, writing a few years after its demolition in 1704. The 4th Earl must have been a man of enterprise, since it was he who carried out the great work of draining the fens in the counties of Northampton, Cambridge, Huntingdon, Norfolk and Lincoln which resulted in "the Bedford Level". Compared with this great undertaking the development of a few acres of his London garden was a comparatively small matter. In 1631 he applied for and obtained from the King the necessary licence to build, a licence which would no doubt have been refused to a less highly placed applicant. Armed with the royal permission, Bedford embarked on his layout, which was conceived on fine, spacious lines with a great central square, the Covent Garden Market of today, and symmetrically disposed streets about it. The general design is said to have been reached with the assistance of Inigo Jones, one of the few men in England thoroughly conversant with the classical towns of Italy; but there is little proof of this, though the church of St. Paul's, of which only the existing great portico is partly original, was certainly his work. The north and

Craven House, Drury Lane

east sides of the square were surrounded by an elegant arcade, of which a rebuilt fragment survives; on the west lay the church; and the south side was closed by the high garden wall of Bedford House.

This area of new houses, so conveniently placed both for Whitehall and the City, became at once the centre of fashionable, if slightly raffish, life. There were many coffee-houses and taverns in the neighbourhood, and a way of living, an amalgamation as it were of Chelsea and Bloomsbury in their best days, developed here in a manner which

15

was not to be found in any other part of the town. Such men as Lely, Kneller, Wycherley, Dr. Arne lived in this new quarter, where such pleasant and intelligent company was so readily available, while Dryden frequented Will's Coffee House, which stood at the corner of Bow Street and Russell Street. It was here that Pope was brought, then aged about ten, at his own request so that he might have a sight of the great poet. A few doors away was Button's rival establishment, which was particularly the gathering place of Swift, Addison and Steele. Much time was spent here in convivial conversation, often five or six hours, according to Pope, who added, "I was of the company for about a year, but found it too much for me. It hurt my health, and so I quitted it." Admiral Russell, Earl of Orford, the victor of La Hogue in 1692 and a nephew of the builder of the square, had a large house in the north-west corner, where he died. The churchyard of St. Paul's contains the bones of many who were famous during the halcyon half century following the Restoration. Samuel Butler was laid there in 1680. "About twenty-five of his old acquaintances at his funeral, I myself being one", wrote Aubrey. John Taylor, the "water-poet", and Wilkes and Thomas King, both famous actors during the reigns of the last Stuart monarchs, lie in this small yard, though there is nothing to mark their graves.

In 1704 Bedford House was demolished, the Russell family having moved to Southampton House on the property they had inherited, as will be later described, in Bloomsbury. Streets were laid out on the site, and the market, which had existed inconspicuously close to the garden wall, was moved into the middle of the square and increased in importance. Commercially this was a success, but inevitably it altered the residential nature of the square. With the open space, which had provided so agreeable a promenade for people of fashion, filled for half the day with barrows and kiosks and the far from refined vendors of fruit and vegetables bawling the merits of their wares, the spacious houses in the piazza were no longer so pleasant to live in. The life of the coffee-houses and of the theatre was unaffected, but the big houses degenerated into inns and lodging houses, and the social centre of London moved farther westward to the fine new squares which will be described in a subsequent chapter.

Owing to Lord Bedford's enterprise the area of Covent Garden developed sooner than the surrounding districts which lay between the legal area of Chancery Lane and the king's park of St. James's. At the time of the Restoration Lincoln's Inn Fields was still an open space of great size, more than double its present area, with houses scattered at random round the verges; while St. Giles Fields were even more pastoral and adjoined completely open meadows and farmlands on its west side. The same could not be said of St. Martin's Fields, for a considerable amount of building had already taken place in the vicinity of the church. From the rising ground on its north side a rural lane with hedges on either side had wound down the gentle slope, skirting the wall of the Convent Gardens, passed close to the west end of the little Gothic structure, and so on to Whitehall. Early in the seventeenth century spasmodic building had begun along this pleasant little road, and in 1630 the Earl of Leicester had obtained a grant of land amongst the meadows on its west side. There he enclosed a large garden, in which he built his house. It was destined to preserve its existence for longer than most of the great houses built during this age. Before the century closed a square was laid out before the south front of Leicester House and was surrounded by solid brick houses planned on spacious, simple lines. Isaac Newton and Hogarth were early residents and Sir Joshua Reynolds and John Hunter lived here some years later. These famous inhabitants are commemorated by four smoke-blackened busts raised on Aberdeen granite bases, one in each corner of the square garden. Reynolds' home, on the west side, was the last of these fine houses to be demolished: its plain, well-proportioned façade and handsome panelled rooms disappearing beneath the housebreakers' picks during the iconoclastic years between the two wars.

This brief survey, then, indicates very roughly the extent of the metropolis at the time of the Restoration. There was at that time, as there has been ever since, an urge to carry purely domestic building ever farther westwards, a *Drang nach Westen*, and if it had not been for the formidable barrier created by the vast enclosed area of the Palace of Westminster, development would probably have occurred along the river bank on its southward reach. But beyond some scattered houses in the western purlieus of Westminster and on Tothill Fields there was little to disturb the rural harmony of the scene. The barns and buildings of Ebury Farm were still surrounded by the rich pastures and arable fields, which with the outlying areas to the north were to yield a precious harvest to the Grosvenor family half a century or so later. Thus a "green belt" a mile or two wide surrounded London on every side, but in the deep countryside beyond this area were to be found a number of attractive villages, ringed like planets round the sun. All were destined to be swallowed up in the spate of building which during the centuries swept out from the "Great Wen", as Cobbett always named it, and completely submerged and obliterated the majority; only a few, such as Chelsea and Hampstead, retained a certain degree of integrity.

There is perhaps a certain melancholy interest in passing swiftly round this chain of pretty, doomed villages, which at the time of the Restoration were on the whole so thriving and so individual. Across the flat Ebury meadows stretched the long, straight road from White-hall to Fulham, where it crossed the Thames and passed through the more undulating country to Kingston and Hampton Court Palace. Thus it linked the two principal royal establishments and was known as the King's Private Road. Charles II constantly travelled back and forth along this road, often, it is said, traversing the twelve miles or so of the journey on foot.

The first village through which the royal route passed was Chelsea, the most elegant and fashionable place of residence in the neighbour-hood of the metropolis. A century after the Restoration it was still described as "a large and populous village, two miles from London", and at the time when Charles walked through it, it consisted of little more than a cluster of houses set about the fourteenth-century church standing close to the banks of the river, with a number of fine houses and large gardens disposed amongst the silver willows and tall trees which grew luxuriantly on the moist soil. The largest of these pleasant country seats was Beaufort House, of which only a length of high brick garden wall, behind the street of that name, survives. It was in a house on this site that Sir Thomas More came to live about 1524 and where he was visited by Erasmus and Holbein. It was then acquired by Henry VIII and became the home of his neglected daughter, Elizabeth, and later of his even more neglected wife, Anne of Cleves, who died here in 1557. Towards the end of the century it was rebuilt by Robert Cecil, Earl of Salisbury, and Kip's view shows how splendid a domain it was, with a long gabled house standing on a terrace amidst courtyards and formal gardens, which must have rivalled any of the great houses in England. The vast building designed by Sir Christopher Wren for old and disabled soldiers was not begun until three years before the end of Charles II's reign; but six years earlier the Apothe-caries Society had leased in the village a site of nearly four acres for the growing of rare plants and herbs. Later this Physic Garden was given to the Society by Sir Hans Sloane, who bought the manor of Chelsea in 1712. Chelsea at the Restoration was only at the beginning of its popularity as a place of residence, a popularity it did not lose even when its entity as a detached village disappeared. Ranelagh Gardens, described in Dodsley's *Environs* of 1761 as "a public place of pleasure not to be equalled in Europe, . . . the resort of people of the first quality", brought it still further into the fashionable world.

Pursuing the King's Road a few miles farther the traveller would come to the village of Fulham, dominated by the ancient palace of the Bishops of London. Here was no modish settlement, no place of villeggiatura for the aristocratic society of London, but a simple, prosperous little community thriving on the fish to be caught in the bountiful river which flowed gently between its wide, shallow banks in a majestic curve round the village, and on the plethora of fruit and vegetables which flourished in the rich mould and loam of the district. Fulham was the kitchen garden for the supply of London, and the produce of its orchards was sold in the booths beneath the walls of Bedford House garden; while the fish, of which there was an exotic assortment, salmon, smelts, lampreys, barbels, and even sturgeon, was also carried to the London markets. In a sheltered position there was even a vineyard which produced a wine said to have resembled Burgundy: "Burgundy type" it would nowadays presumably be labelled.

Two or three miles to the north of this English Garden of Eden, on ground rising from the low-lying meadows of the Thames valley, was the hamlet of Kensington. As yet it had no aura of royalty, for it was not until 1689 that William III bought the building originally known as Kensington House from Lord Nottingham and with Wren's assistance converted it into a modest palace. The salubrious air and open situation suited the asthmatic condition of the king, who suffered severely from the smoke, mists and foul vapours which drifted about Whitehall. Until the king's arrival in the village the principal seat in the parish had been the strange Renaissance house once known as Cope Castle after its first owner, Sir Walter Cope. At the Restoration, however, the Copes had disappeared from the scene and the property had passed into the possession of Lord Holland, later Earl of Warwick; the name of the house was then changed to that which the blackened ruins still retain. These were a few of the pleasant villages lying on the west side of the metropolis; farther north, beyond Paddington, the rather portentous name given to a few cottages and a church standing close to the fields of Marybone Farm, the ground rose steeply and on the crown of the long escarpment stood the twin villages of Hampstead and Highgate. The excellent air of these bracing heights had long made them highly popular places of residence, while the superb and distant prospect in every direction, and particularly over the town crowded in the valley, was unsurpassed near London, except, perhaps, by the panorama from the summit of the royal park at Greenwich. In addition the mineral waters, which came to the surface at Hampstead, provided a conveniently placed purgative source for those suffering from the excesses of the metropolis. Its popularity with the "good-timers" proved its undoing, and in 1709 Macky protested that there were "so many loose women . . . that modest company are ashamed to appear here". Fortunately the loose women seem to have kept to the pumproom, and as places of residence these well timbered hill-tops never lost their desirability.

Hampstead and Highgate have retained their charm to so great a degree that it is surprising to reflect that Hackney, to the south-east, beyond Sir Hugh Myddleton's New River Head in the fields of Islington, once excelled them both as an elegant place of abode; indeed it rivalled Chelsea. There seems little in its situation, save the meadows bordering the river Lea, to account for its popularity though its convenient vicinity to the City may have been a factor, for it was rather those rich men whose lives centred round the Exchange who here made their homes, than the aristocrats who passed their days at Court. The large number of horses which were daily hired to make the journey between the City and this rich village led to their being named Hackney horses, and this name soon passed to public coaches and chairs. According to Maitland there were no more than twenty-five of these useful vehicles plying for hire in 1625, but in 1662 this number had increased to four hundred. A century later there was double this number, and elaborate regulations for their licensing, much as are in force today, had been drawn up by the Hackney Coach Office, which was started in 1696. The northern chain of villages ended with Stratford le Bow, on the banks of the river Lea, which for much of its course forms the boundary between Middlesex and Essex, and falls into the Thames a short way to the east of the Isle of Dogs.

South of the Thames the villages were less favoured residentially and had little of the social grace of those to the north, with however the partial exception of the two lying on the river at either end of the southern arc: Greenwich to the east and, to a lesser degree, Battersea to the west. The air of the Kent and Surrey bank had the reputation

The Bayswater Road, about 1800: from a drawing by Paul Sandby

Hackney Ford in the eighteenth century

Islington

Camberwell

Highgate

"PLANET" VILLAGES

of being insalubrious, even Chamberlayne, a blatant propagandist for the metropolis and its neighbourhood, wrote "The villages seated on the South Side are noted to be unhealthy, in regard to the vapours drawn from them by the Sun." It was extraordinary what ills were credited to the rare and gentle English sun; so undesirable was it considered that for centuries every house turned its back upon it. Like the black night air, it had so far as possible to be excluded from every room. Royal Greenwich as it had been since the fifteenth century, when Humphrey, Duke of Gloucester, Henry IV's youngest son, had erected his palace here of Placentia or Pleasaunce, was one of the most historic places near London. At the Restoration the rambling Tudor buildings, in which Henry VIII's two daughters had been born and in which his son had died, were subsiding into the soft mud on which they were built, and only the Queen's House, standing on the rising slope of the park, provided suitable accommodation for a monarch. Great changes were to be seen here during the following half-century: Webb's Palladian range, Wren's domes and arcades, and Vanbrugh's courts were to form a microcosm of the work of the finest Stuart architects, but at Charles's return there was little to bring residents here, and there was no more than a cluster of houses round the disjointed palace buildings. The adjacent village of Deptford, lying beyond the stream of the Ravinsbourne, was very different in character. Since early times shipbuilding had been carried on here, and the river front presented perpetually a busy scene with a throng of buildings crowding to the water's edge and, in front of them, the wharfs and quays of Admiralty and commercial docks. It was Evelyn's house at Deptford, Sayes Court, that Peter the Great rented in 1698 when he came over to study and take part in the work of shipbuilding in the King's Yard. He proved a rough and unsatisfactory tenant both to the owner and his staff. A member of the latter wrote discouragingly to Evelyn during the Czar's stay: "There is a house full of people, and right nasty. . . . The King is expected here this day; the best parlour is pretty clean for him to be entertained in." It was with the utmost relief that Evelyn heard of his distinguished tenant's departure. Pepys in his official capacity was often at Deptford; and also in a private capacity, in ardent and often successful pursuit of "la femme Bagwell".

Westward lay Camberwell, a village of no particular interest, but made attractive by the groves of trees in which it was set and the thickly wooded slopes of Denmark Hill rising to the south of it. On higher ground, above the fields of Piddos Farm, was Clapham, destined to become a place of some residential distinction during the eighteenth century. From the hills of Clapham a winding road led down the gentle slope to Battersea, lying in the flat meadows by the river bank. Had it been more easily accessible from Whitehall it might, in spite of the doubtful air, have enjoyed the same popularity as Chelsea, directly across the water, but the Thames formed a formidable barrier when the only bridges were London Bridge, three or four miles away down stream, and Fulham, a couple of miles in the other direction. Amongst the group of cottages lay the spreading Tudor manor-house of the St. John family, in which the great Lord Bolingbroke was born in 1678. It was already in poor repair when Bolingbroke wrote to his brother in 1743 : "I have had an estimate made of the Repairs necessary to keep this old house on its legs for my time." The house indeed lasted for his lifetime and twenty-seven years longer, but in 1778 all but one wing was demolished, and in 1925 this last remnant, which had been incorporated into a flour mill, was destroyed. The family, however, left an architectural mark on the village, for in 1699 Bolingbroke's father, Henry St. John, built the Terrace House as a dower house for his wife. It was designed in the comfortable style usually connected with Wren's name, though in fact the number of private houses built from his designs was very small indeed. The house still stands, though modern buildings crowd closely round it and all but a patch of the garden, which originally stretched to the water's edge, has been covered with streets and houses. Development in this locality was not swift, so that during the latter half of the eighteenth century, William Curtis, the botanist, was still able to find in Battersea Fields many of the specimens which he recorded in his magnificent work *Flora Londinensis*.

This, then, concludes the ambit of the planet villages as they were at the Restoration, lying in or on the verge of "the pleasant evergreen valley" through which the river wound its gentle, devious course. Within a century or two these attractive hamlets were with greater or lesser violence to be absorbed into the photosphere of the central body, until the whole system became the spreading, sprawling city we know today.

II

The Houses of the Great

During the reigns of the Tudor monarchs the path from power and riches to an unmarked grave beneath the stone-paved floor of the church of St. Peter ad Vincula, within the precincts of the Tower, was remarkably well trodden. One after another this short but painful journey was made by men who, having achieved wealth and distinction through the lavish largesse of the crowned head, had thought their position unassailable and had overreached themselves. With stunning swiftness the elaborate structure of a life, which had been built up with care and perspicacity, was shattered, and the victim would find himself at an uncomfortable elevation above the crowd on Tower Hill with only a few minutes at his disposal in which to make a graceful and moving exit from the scene. Like a procession of the English counties the holders of great names passed to their doom—Buckingham, Essex, Somerset, Northumberland, Norfolk, Surrey followed the familiar road to the miserable climax. The destination was the same, while the point of departure varied very little. In almost every case the journey started from one of the vast rambling houses on the banks of the Thames between the City and Whitehall. The courts, buildings and gardens which had been animated with the throng of a great household must have become suddenly silent as the central figure round which the whole organization revolved was so ominously and suddenly removed to the dungeons of the Tower. To the host of retainers the loss of their master and the probable sale of the house represented a disaster, but to the populace these constant executions were a cheap and welcome public entertainment. The higher the position of the victim, the greater the interest of the spectacle; and undoubtedly some of the popularity of the Tudor despots with the common people was due to their ruthless treatment of the nobility. Pride and rapacity became supportable qualities when they were almost certain to be followed by a violent fall.

Thus justice or royal revenge was constantly creating changes of ownership amongst the line of riverside houses, and with change of owner came change of name, so that the perpetual alteration from one territorial appellation to another is apt to be bewildering. Usually it is the name of the last owner which remains attached to the site in the names of the streets, alleys and court which eventually covered the area of the house and garden. At the time of the Restoration these houses with illustrious names were, in general, as doomed as single residential entities as their owners had been in earlier generations. As has been seen, the centre of rich and fashionable life was beginning to move elsewhere, and a rowdy element, attracted by taverns and dubious places of amusement, was invading this aristocratic area. Few of the houses were of great architectural merit: the majority consisted of as haphazard a group of buildings as the Palace of Whitehall itself, though their extent was far smaller. The original medieval or Tudor buildings, which usually formed the nucleus of the house, had a modestly defensive air with perhaps a tower or two and a battlemented wall facing the river, as at Durham House. To this robust body would be added long ranges of timber-framed buildings as the owner required more accommodation for himself, his retainers, or his horses. The buildings developed at random round courtyards as occasion demanded, and the resultant group resembled somewhat the old inns to be found in many country towns today, with an archway opening from the street and long unsymmetrical wings running back on either side of a court. In the greater number of inns, however, the front to the street was rebuilt in Georgian times.

Arundel House, lying between Essex House and Somerset House, was an example of this casual growth. It had previously been known as Seymour Place until the execution of its owner, the Lord High Admiral of England, when it was bought by the Earl of Arundel, whose son, the Duke of Norfolk, was also destined for the block. Though it covered a great area, there was no attempt at splendour and magnificence in the exterior of the buildings, such as was to be seen in Cardinal Wolsey's vast new house on the banks of the Thames at Hampton: rather it resembled a village of independent but adjoining houses set round a wide courtyard. On the north side stood a fine hall constructed in stone with a central louvre in the roof and three long Gothic windows looking on to the court. On either side was a jumble of picturesque buildings, some of one story, some of three, some with timbered gables, some, dating probably from about 1600, with orderly brick fronts and neatly arranged rows of lattice windows. On the river side was a battlemented brick tower from which there was a distant view along the broad curve of the Thames. On the rise of Ludgate Hill to the north-east could be seen the great mass of St. Paul's Cathedral, its strange truncated tower and incongruous classical façade rising far above the roofs of the intervening houses. The busy waterfront stretched away to London Bridge, where the long procession of low arches supporting their eccentric superstructure closed the river view. But beyond the bridge could be descried the massive four-square walls of the Tower with a glimpse of open country beyond. This was how Hollar portrayed the scene before the Great Fire and the subsequent rebuilding altered the whole aspect of the City.

It was at his house in the Strand that Thomas, Earl of Arundel, assembled his remarkable collection of marbles. Lord Arundel had advised Charles I on the purchase of pictures; he was equally an authority on sculpture. In search of the antique he despatched John Evelyn to Rome and William Petty to Greece and Smyrna, a discerning choice of buyers by whose efforts he found himself, at enormous cost, the possessor of thirty-seven statues, one hundred and twenty-eight busts, and two hundred and fifty marbles, the majority dating from the best periods and of superb quality. Lord Arundel died in Padua in 1646, and twenty-three years later Evelyn was deeply distressed at finding the collection "miserably neglected, and scattered up and down about the garden and other parts of Arundel House, and how exceedingly the corrosive air of London impaired them". Without delay he persuaded the then owner, Henry Howard, to offer the marbles, but not the statues, to the University of Oxford, who accepted them with alacrity. The statues were sold in 1720, but in the interval they had been sadly mutilated, and a large number had been pilfered by a gardener at Arundel House, who had set them up in a public garden he had opened in Southwark, and thus had tastefully adorned his little pleasure resort at very small cost to his own pocket.

Not all the houses were as devoid of architectural distinction and symmetry as Arundel House. There was, for instance, Somerset House, which is the only one of this line of noble houses to retain its identity, though it was entirely reconstructed from the designs of Sir William Chambers in the years following 1776. It was originally built by Lord Protector Somerset, who, it is perhaps needless to say, lost his head on Tower Hill in 1552, at the moment when his splendid new house was nearing completion. Before this unhappy ending to his career, he had utilized his dominant position to acquire the houses, or inns as they were generally called, of five bishops, Chester, Landaff, Lichfield, Coventry and Worcester. Having successfully dispossessed these prelates, he found himself with a spacious and magnificent site at the apex of the wide curve of the river. The building he erected, which was set back from the water on a terrace above a formal garden, showed the most enlightened taste. It was usually supposed to have been built by John of Padua, who was also credited with the design of Longleat in Wiltshire. This obscure figure was raised to fame by Horace Walpole on the flimsiest evidence, much of which has now been disproved, but until this century the Italian immigrant solved many architectural problems. There now seems no answer as to who in 1547 could have devised a building which led Stow early in the seventeenth century to write: "The first Court of Somerset House next the Strand . . . affords us a view of the first dawning of taste in England, this being the only fabric that I know deviates from the Gothic, or imitates the manner of the ancients." Stow had only a few years to wait before he saw Inigo Jones's even greater masterpiece arise in Whitehall. With Somerset's head successfully in the bag, his fine mansion became the property of the Crown, and was used as a palace for dowager queens of England. Anne of Denmark spent her widowhood here, and Henrietta Maria came here on the Restoration and remained until the outbreak of the plague, when she returned to France; it was the residence of Catherine of Braganza for seven years. The interior was no less handsome than the exterior and contained a large number of fine rooms, which Pepys found "most stately and nobly furnished" when he visited them in 1665. When, in 1775, George III purchased for Queen Charlotte Buckingham House, which will be described later, Somerset was no longer required as a royal dower house. The old building was then demolished and a new erected, which was devised for other purposes.

The "inns" of the bishops, which at one time were a great feature of the Thames waterfront, seem to have exercised an irresistible attraction over kings and protectors. As we have seen, Somerset seized five at a single swoop, while Henry VIII had snaffled Wolsey's modest home in Whitehall. Perhaps the finest of the "inns" with the exception of Whitehall was Durham House, which had originally been built by Bishop Thomas Hatfield in the middle of the fourteenth century and presented a handsome, battlemented façade to the river. To Henry VIII it clearly appeared too ambitious a building for a bishop, even for the prince bishop of Durham, and he effected an "exchange" with the then holder of the see, Cuthbert Tonstall. It is not apparent what, if anything, constituted the royal contribution to the bargain. The King made good use of the house and garden he had

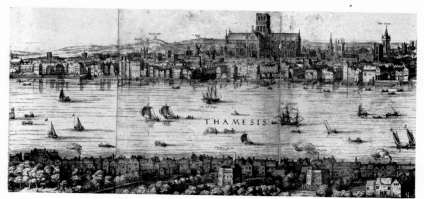

The River Front and Old St. Paul's

Suffolk House, Charing Cross (later Northumberland House)

Arundel House, Strand

THAMES-SIDE BUILDINGS IN THE EARLY SEVENTEENTH
CENTURY

The Three Stages of Somerset House: medieval, seventeenth century
and eighteenth century

so easily acquired as a place for festivities, feasts and jousts, and he no doubt soon dispelled any clerical atmosphere which may have hung about the medieval walls. On the king's death, Edward VI gave it to his sister Elizabeth, who in her turn bestowed it on Sir Walter Raleigh. On the Queen's death the house, which seems to have been reduced to a sad state of repair, was returned to the see of Durham. As a residence its existence was finished, and about 1640 part of the area was laid out in one of the speculative housing schemes, such as were to cover the majority of these fine houses and gardens. The tenements round Durham Yard seem to have been unusually badly constructed and squalid, since a century after their construction they were already almost in ruin. This miserable area, with the steep slope to the river covered with crumbling hovels, was in 1768 acquired by the Adam brothers, as will be later described, and here their superb, but unprofitable, terraces and streets arose, the greater part of which were to be allowed little more than a century and a half of existence.

It forms melancholy reading the rise and swift destruction of these great buildings which lined the Thames bank. If by some strange chance they had been preserved, if for some reason prosperity and commerce had deserted the City of London and the town had ceased to develop, we should have found ourselves with a sweep of river which could rival the Grand Canal at Venice. The architecture was far less sophisticated, but the spread of water was far grander and wider, while the buildings were much lower. The proportions thus were different, and perhaps more impressive. When Canaletto painted his radiant scenes of the Thames, in the middle of the eighteenth century, the early buildings had mostly disappeared, but the beauty of the panorama, as he saw it, seems to have stimulated him to a brilliance of execution which he seldom equalled when painting his native waters. One house, and one alone if we except Somerset, which had changed its function, survived until the second half of the nineteenth century, and this was Northumberland House. For more than two centuries the long, rather severe façade, with its flanking towers and a lion standing on a central superstructure, faced the junction of streets at the top of Whitehall. For its last years it enjoyed a wide view over the great new square which was laid out in the years following 1829 on the site of the Royal Mews; but in 1874, the reigning duke having reluctantly agreed to its sale for a sum of half a million, the house was demolished and Northumberland Avenue, one of the gloomiest streets in London, was laid out on its site.

Owing to its late survival Northumberland House is the only one of the great Strand houses the appearance of which both within and without is well known. The Jacobean elevation to the street was impressive and was originally surmounted by a cresting formed of a motto in stone. In 1618, however, the letter S fell and killed a young man standing below, and this unusual catastrophe probably led to the replacement of these dangerous letters by a balustrade. The façade to the garden which was rebuilt in the eighteenth century was plain and austere, but concealed within its formidable walls fine rooms with richly decorated ceilings. The staircase rising from the entrance hall was considered very "noble", with its marble treads, ormolu balustrade and mahogany handrail; it formed a fitting prelude and approach to the gallery, which was a hundred feet in length and contained a collection of old masters displayed on its damask walls which the National Gallery across the square might well have envied. The whole house, which embraced over a hundred and fifty rooms, was dark and gloomy, and seems to have been little used by its owners during the last years of its existence.

The exterior of the house was familiar to all Londoners, but few were ever allowed to set foot within its august portals. In 1851, however, to celebrate the Great Exhibition the house was unexpectedly thrown open to the public and huge crowds thronged the great rooms, the splendour of which was so soon to be turned to rubble and dust by the picks of the housebreakers. Great astonishment was caused by the garden: not only was it far larger than anyone had supposed, although it had lost its river frontage by the formation of the Embankment, but also its aspect was such as no one had anticipated. Trim lawns, gravel paths and many shaped flower-beds might have been expected to form the Victorian "pleasaunce" of this ducal mansion, but instead of ordered decorum there was a rampant and luxuriant wilderness. Within the sheltering and concealing walls, trees and shrubs, hawthorns and hazels, had grown uncontrolled and unchecked into a deep, almost impenetrable jungle, so that the house rose from amidst the dark and tangled growth like the palace of a Sleeping Beauty. Only a few yards from this wild oasis, the spacious and grandiose design of Trafalgar Square was swiftly reaching completion.

Thus one after another the great houses, which had once formed a constant chain from the City to Whitehall, disappeared, link by link, before the encroachment of humble buildings. The Stuart nobles were moving to other sites, perhaps less picturesque, since the river has always provided one of the most beautiful panoramas in London, but at least more isolated. No longer would they have to endure the obscene sounds which wafted over their garden walls from the taverns, and worse, which had grown up in their once exclusive district, nor the jeers of a vulgar populace that met them as they left their gateways. The houses on the stretch of river bank from the City to Charing Cross were clearly doomed, but at the southern extremity of the chain the area in Whitehall took on a new phase of fashionable life.

After the destruction of Whitehall Palace by fire in 1698 and King William's eventual decision not to raise a new royal dwelling on the site, an agreeable area, with an aura of unusual distinction, was available for private building. Here several houses of considerable size were constructed, of which the most important was Richmond House, while Montagu House adjoined; both rose on the edge of what had been the Privy Garden in the days of the palace. The former house stood, appropriately enough, on the former site of the apartments of Louise de Querouaille, Duchess of Portsmouth, the mother of the first Duke of Richmond. These were the lodgings which had so greatly shocked Evelyn when he accompanied the King thither in 1683. The Duchess had just left her bed and her maids were combing her hair, while the King and other admirers stood round. But it was the furnishings, not the lady, which interested Evelyn: the panels of tapestry on the walls, with silver sconces between them; the gilded clocks and chimney ornaments; rich china vases and Japan cabinets, which were a new and rare introduction; silver plate on the tables and some of the finest pictures from the royal collections on any vacant area of wall. The rooms were far more magnificent than the apartments of the neglected queen. The site, therefore, had a sentimental interest for the second Duke of Richmond, who owed so much to the shrewdness of his grandmother. The house is said to have been designed by Lord Burlington, but it was not destined long to endure. In 1791 it was burnt to the ground, and though rebuilt was finally demolished in 1819 when Richmond Terrace was erected on its site.

In spite of its short existence there are two reasons why its memory should survive: firstly Canaletto painted one of his most attractive pictures of the river scene from its terrace; and secondly it was a forerunner by a decade of the Royal Academy as an art school. The third duke opened his gallery of pictures and statues to students, and provided Cipriani and Wilton to instruct in painting and sculpture respectively, without charge. On an adjacent and equally favoured site between the river and the Privy Garden was Montagu House, whither the family of that name migrated from their house in Blooms-bury, which will shortly be described. It was less ambitious than Richmond House and in 1860 was replaced by a grandiose building in the uncongenial Françoise I manner, a style which still gives a distant flavour of the less attractive aspects of the Loire valley to the southern reaches of Hyde Park Corner.

About half a century before these two fine houses were built, a certain amount of development had taken place on the far side of the royal precincts of Whitehall in a short street leading towards St. James's Park. Here in the years following the Restoration Sir George Downing had built, on a piece of land he had received from the King, a row of plain and serviceable houses in a simple, straightforward style of which many were to rise in later Stuart London. Three still survive and have achieved an eminence which their architecture hardly warrants. At least it is to be hoped that the street now retains none of the equivocal reputation which was borne by its founder, for the name George Downing was used by the inhabitants of New England in much the same way as the name Quisling is used in these days. Downing went out to New England with his parents in 1638 and became the second graduate of Harvard, but his political duplicity and avaricious character, which were apparent in his public life in England, earned him the hatred of the people amongst whom he had spent his youth.

Eligible sites in Whitehall were exceedingly rare and in any case seldom provided space for a great layout of house, pavilions and courtyards which post-Restoration noblemen considered essential for their London houses. The architects of the period, and their number was few, devised no plan, no special layout, for a great house in Lon-don. Either it was a house in a street, with a frontage rather wider than its neighbours, or it was designed as a house in the country, where there was no limit, except expense, to the spreading nature of its plan. The only concession made in the building of these houses was to erect a wall on the street side of the entrance courtyard in the place of an iron *claire voie*, which in the country would have kept the deer of the park at bay. On the Continent, and particularly in France, the technique of designing and planning town houses reached a high art: so high, indeed, that particularly during the reign of Louis XV there was a tendency to build country houses as if they had been situated in what are now the Third or Seventh *arrondissements* of Paris. The French plan, which became a convention, though its details were subtly adjusted to the site, consisted of a house built round a courtyard, which was entered by a carriage-way through the wing fronting the street. The range facing the entrance arch usually contained the principal rooms, while at the side were dependencies for staff, with extensive stables in the fourth wing. Many houses designed on these lines are still to be seen in the old quarters of Paris and on a rather less ambitious scale in Bordeaux and Dijon. Thus complete seclusion was achieved on a site which was often of no very great size. This form of planning was seldom attempted in London, though a house in Arlington Street, now demolished, was arranged somewhat on these lines, and Bath House in Piccadilly shows a nineteenth-century version of the French arrangement. In Italy much the same form is found as in France. The Roman nobles were free from that passion for seclusion which forced their English equals to isolate their houses from adjacent inhabitants and to conceal them from the street behind high walls. The great palazzi of Rome such as the Farnesi, the Doria or the Colonna, rise directly from the footway, while their gigantic façades rub shoulders contentedly with the modest homes of humble neighbours.

Banished from the river bank, the nearest convenient area for building was in the neighbourhood of the Duke of Bedford's elegant new *piazza* in Covent Garden, and here, principally along the sweeping pastoral curves of Drury Lane, a number of houses had been built before the Restoration. Amongst these was Drury House which with its gardens and forecourt covered a large area. Probably before the Commonwealth the house was acquired by Lord Craven, but it was not until 1673 that he petitioned for, and received, permission to build a new house on the site and to lay out several streets on the outer perimeter of the unnecessarily spacious garden. Lord Craven was an enthusiastic builder: in the country he erected the tall, tower-like house, Ashdown, on a desolate spur of the Berkshire downs; he converted a rather modest manor-house at Hampstead Marshall into a splendid mansion of great size; while at Coombe Abbey, in Warwickshire, he reconstructed a great part of the gabled Tudor buildings in a handsome Carolean style. Though he lived to the age of almost ninety, his life covering nearly the whole of the seventeenth century, his building enterprises were still incomplete at his death. The accomplished architects John Webb and Captain Wynne were employed on his country houses: the former at Ashdown, the latter at the two others;

but there is no record of the designer of Craven House and its aspect gave little clue. It was a massive, compact building rising to four stories with dormers in the roof above a deep cornice. Between the windows were pilasters supporting cornices which ran between each floor.

Craven, who was a man of remarkable character, is chiefly remembered as an ardent supporter of royal causes. Not only did he give great service to Charles II, both financially and politically, but he also rendered constant assistance to the exiled Queen of Bohemia. His interest in the queen, who was twelve years his senior, was not merely political, and it was commonly rumoured, though probably without truth, that they had been married during Craven's years of exile with Charles II. On the Restoration, the Queen, who was the youngest daughter of James I and so Charles's aunt, expected the offer of a royal lodging in England; but none was forthcoming, and it was to Lord Craven's house in Drury Lane that this neglected lady, who was to prove so vital a link in the descent of the English monarchy, came. In 1662 she moved to Leicester House, half a mile away, and there a fortnight later she died. Her connection with the site of Craven House was not forgotten, for a century or so after her death, when the once magnificent building, which had succeeded that in which the Queen stayed, had descended the social ladder to become a collection of tenements and an inn, it was the Queen of Bohemia's portrait that appeared as a sign over the door of the latter. The Earl died at Craven House in 1697 and his heirs soon after moved their London home to the pastoral fields of Bayswater, where the name still survives. Meanwhile Old Craven House, bereft of all outbuildings and gardens carried on its miserable existence, becoming ever more squalid and more decayed until the early years of the nineteenth century, when it was finally demolished.

The building of Leicester House in the fields to the west of the decayed church of St. Martin has been mentioned in the first chapter. It was a plain brick building, nine windows wide and two stories high, with an attic above, but its position, with an entrance court in front opening on to the spacious square and large garden on the north side, was extremely pleasant; so it is not surprising that it sheltered a succession of distinguished tenants, though it remained in the possession of the Lords Leicester and their heirs until late in the eighteenth century, when it was sold and demolished. Evelyn visited Lady Sunderland at Leicester House in 1679 and was present at an alarming performance by one Richardson of fire-eating. The entertainment consisted principally of the feat of swallowing a variety of flaming and singularly indigestible substances: brimstone and coal, molten glass, a disgusting mixture of pitch, wax and sulphur melted together. Evelyn might well call his achievements "prodigious". Later both the French and the Russian ambassadors made their home here, but it was in the eighteenth century that it received the name of "the Pouting Place of Princes". It was here that George II, when Prince of Wales, lived during the estrangement from his father, and here also Frederick, Prince of Wales, held his court till his death in 1751. George II made no attempt to visit his son's deathbed, indeed was quite unmoved by the calamity of his early demise. "Ach, Fritz ist todt," he remarked casually to his card partners, when informed of the death, and then continued with his game. The widowed Princess remained at Leicester House until 1766, when she moved to Carlton House, but her eldest son lived in the adjacent Saville House until his accession as George III. In the rebuilt Saville House Mary Linwood exhibited her remarkable needlework pictures from 1800 until her death forty-five years later. She specialized in copies of the old masters and her rendering of Carlo Dolci's "Salvator Mundi" was generally considered her masterpiece, though it was closely rivalled by "The Judgement of Cain", which was the product of ten years' work.

Within a few years of the Restoration the area round St. Martin's church ceased to be suitable for the building of houses on a major scale. There was a tendency for gardens to become hemmed in by houses of a less august nature, and there was none of that easy access to the open country which Stuart noblemen seemed to require. Two admirable areas, which suitably combined a convenient propinquity to the heart of the town with a rural spaciousness, were the fields lying to the north of Holborn, and, a little more remote, the open farmland on the north side of the road to Reading, or Piccadilly as it was soon to be called.

The Bloomsbury fields were particularly advantageously placed, since they were equidistant from the City and Whitehall, perhaps a mile and a half from each, while northwards the open country stretched away to the villages of Hampstead and Highgate nestling on their wooded ridge. Thomas Wriothesley, Earl of Southampton, seems to have had the intention of building in these pleasant meadows before the outbreak of the Civil Wars, for in 1636 he applied for a licence to demolish his house in Holborn, cover the site with small houses, and to build a new Southampton House in a different situation. Permission, however, was refused, and it was not until sixteen momentous years had passed that he was allowed to do as he wished. That he should have received any favours during the Commonwealth was remarkable, since he had been a staunch supporter of Charles I and was bitterly opposed to Cromwell, going so far, indeed, as to leave his house at Titchfield in Hampshire when Cromwell announced his intention of visiting him there. He had paid heavy fines for his fidelity to the King, but nevertheless about 1656 he was able to start building a splendid new house in Bloomsbury. It was a long, well-proportioned building consisting of a *piano nobile* with one floor above and a balustrade partially concealing the roof. Two single-storied wings extended forward and the entrance courtyard was separated from the road by a high wall with a majestic central gate. Samuel Scott painted an attractive picture of the house as it appeared in the eighteenth century, with the spacious square surrounded by large brick houses, houses clearly intended for people of the highest quality, to the south of it. The mansion seems to have been freshly completed when Pepys came to see it in 1662 and considered it "a very great and noble work". Three years later Evelyn came to dine with the Lord Treasurer and noted that "he was building a noble square, or piazza, a little town". The name of the architect is unknown, beyond the usual, and in this case impossible, attribution to Inigo Jones. It may well have been the work of John Webb or perhaps of Hugh May; there were few others at that time capable of producing so accomplished a design.

The Lord Treasurer died, leaving no son, in 1667, and the house with the manors of Bloomsbury and St. Giles in the Fields became the property of his daughter Rachel, who was married to William, Lord Russell, son of the Earl, later Duke, of Bedford. The sad history of this devoted couple is well known: how Lord Russell was convicted of complicity in the Rye House Plot and, in spite of his wife's desperate efforts to save his life, was executed in Lincoln's Inn Fields in 1683. Lady Russell lived for another thirty years, addressing her copious and rather melancholy correspondence either from Southampton House or from Stratton, her house in Hampshire. It was at the former that she died, when all her property passed to her son the second Duke of Bedford. In 1732 the name of the house was changed to Bedford House; in 1800 it was demolished and a large number of streets laid out on the site.

Nearly ten years before Lord Russell's death his brother-in-law, Ralph Montagu, began to build a large house on a neighbouring

34

site of thirty-one acres. Montagu, who became later Earl and Duke, married the half-sister of Lady Russell, and this agreeable Bloomsbury building site probably represented part of her inheritance. Montagu, who was ambassador in Paris and a man of great taste and wealth and also, according to Macaulay, "a faithless and shameless one", intended his new house to surpass all others in London in magnificence. He engaged as architect Robert Hooke, the assistant of Wren, who also advised on the work. In 1680 the house was more or less complete and Evelyn, who was almost as indefatigable as Celia Fiennes in visiting houses, inspected the new building and made careful notes of his impressions. He was not unduly enthusiastic about the exterior: the courtyard seemed a little meagre, which was uncalled for when the site was so spacious. House and garden covered eight acres, while the

Montagu House, Bloomsbury : the Entrance Front

remainder of the site was wooded meadowland, which framed the attractive prospect to the northern heights. The effects of Montagu's residence in the French capital, though he seems in fact to have spent more of his time in supervising his house than his mission, were to be seen in the architecture which was "after the French pavilion way" and thus rather suspect, but of the interior Evelyn was full of praise. He was much impressed by the magnificent stair with walls painted by Verrio, which led to a suite of rooms of the greatest richness and splendour, all of which were also embellished with Verrio's Olympian scenes. The contents, pictures, furniture and marbles were more than worthy of their setting; thus Montagu had probably achieved his objective and surpassed all, or almost all, other great London houses in elegance and grandeur. His satisfaction was of short duration.

One night in January 1686 Lady Russell in Southampton House woke to hear strange sounds in the Square. She sent a servant to enquire what was amiss, and was told that Montagu House was on fire. So fiercely did it burn that flames and sparks flew over Bedford

House, to its imminent danger, and thick smoke filled the house and almost stifled one of the Russell children. By five o'clock in the morning Montagu House was completely consumed: the fine building and priceless contents were reduced to a heap of rubble and ashes. This disaster must have been a sad reverse for Hooke whose finest achievement, one on which he had expended infinite care as appears from his diary, was thus annihilated in the short space of five hours. But for a wealthy and enthusiastic builder such as Montagu it was merely a stimulant to produce something even more splendid, and an opportunity of avoiding any errors he may have detected in his first house. The courtyard, for example, would be more spacious, but the French flavour of the building was to be far more strongly marked. Hooke was not invited to superintend the birth of the phoenix: instead Montagu called in a French architect to supply plans and French wall painters to decorate the interior. Pierre Puget is said, on the authority of Campbell's *Vitruvius Britannicus*, to have been Montagu's curious choice of an architect, but whether in fact *le Michel-Ange provençal* provided the plans for the building, which was destined to become the first British Museum, is likely to remain for ever in the mists. The planning of the house showed little inspiration or invention: on the ground floor were a dozen spacious rectangular rooms, and on the floor above an equal number, similar in area but rather higher, approached by a broad and easy stair. It received little of the praise which had been lavished on Hooke's building, and with its long flights of communicating rooms must have been devoid of domestic comfort. It was, at least in plan, more suited to the purpose to which it was eventually put.

On the death of Sir Hans Sloane in 1753 it was found that his magnificent collection, which had cost over £50,000 was to be offered to the nation for £20,000. This was at once accepted, and at the same time it was decided to purchase the Cottonian Library, and the Harleian manuscripts from Lord Oxford for £10,000, which with the Sloane collection were to form the nucleus of a British Museum. The raising of these large sums and also a substantial endowment fund presented no difficulties: it was effected without cost to the taxpayer by promoting a lottery, and this great national institution was thus raised on a basis of hazard. No less than £300,000 was obtained, and the only problem which was difficult of solution was how to find a building suitable for the display of these priceless objects. A few years earlier the second Duke of Montagu had died in his house in the Privy Garden at Whitehall, having already apparently moved there from Bloomsbury; and his daughter and heir, Lady Cardigan, accepted an offer to sell Montagu House for the purpose of the Museum.

For this "large and magnificent building, finely ornamented with paintings, situated in the most convenient part of the whole town, and having an extensive garden of near eight acres", as it was contemporaneously described, the modest price was £10,000. It is interesting to note how drastically the balance of the metropolis has altered in two centuries: in the middle of the eighteenth century Bloomsbury was considered as central as Piccadilly Circus today. The decorative treatment of the interior is carefully described, room by room, in the *Gentleman's Magazine* of June 1814. Though the terms used are rather obscure it is clear that the most lavish embellishments were to be found on the grand staircase, "easy and capacious, rich iron scroll fence", and in the Grand Saloon, which was the central room on the first floor overlooking the garden. On the walls of the stair were lively scenes in plaster "basso-relievos of Roman battles, trophies, and Bacchanalian revels"; while the ceiling was painted by La Fosse and Rousseau with "Time and Eternity, centrical, surrounded by the gods and goddesses" who were indulging in their usual junketings. About the Saloon the description waxes somewhat incoherent in its eulogies: "This central burst of magnificence", the writer exclaims "is a trial of art, and that of the true sublime and beautiful." Montagu was one of the few London houses that Celia Fiennes visited, though she was indefatigable in inspecting country houses. She also was impressed by the central saloon, but rather for its rather dangerous acoustic properties than for any other reason. "One roome in the middle of the building", she wrote, "is of a surpriseing height curiously painted and very large, yet soe contrived that speake very low to the wall or wanscoate in one corner and it should be heard with advantage in the very opposite corner across."

Unfortunately the handsome decoration of the interior cannot have formed a very suitable background to the interesting but not always very ornamental objects displayed. On the gallery of the grand staircase, for example, stood three stuffed giraffes, their primordial forms contrasting uncomfortably with the sophisticated Palladian decoration. In 1823 Robert Smirke's austere building was begun and in 1852 Montagu House was demolished and Smirke's pilastered and porticoed façade gradually covered the site.

Southampton and Montagu were the most important of the Bloomsbury mansions, but there were others of lesser size in this favoured locality such as Thanet House; there were also the streets and squares of substantial houses, which will be described later. At the Restoration it was already becoming difficult to obtain large areas of land fronting the main road of a suitably extensive size for the construction of houses in the country style with space for the complicated appurtenances of stables, outbuildings and gardens. Thus it was to the less fashionable area of Piccadilly that rich noblemen turned; and here rose a line of splendid houses, Burlington, Clarendon, Berkeley, Clarges, each set in a large area of ground with formal gardens enclosed by high walls extending away to the open fields to the north. Of these great buildings Clarendon House probably surpassed even Montagu House in splendour as much as it undoubtedly did in the beauty of its architecture. While Piccadilly was merely a country road leading to the little village of Kensington and on into the west country, it was unnecessary for it to be given any particular name, but the eastern length, where there were a few small houses, was generally known as Portugal Street. How the name the street now holds arose is uncertain but it would seem probable that it comes from the word peccadilloes, the name given to the lace and frills worn by men during the reigns of the two first Stuart kings, and which also formed an essential part of male costume during Charles II's reign. In any case, as the street increased in importance and perhaps in part owing to the unpopularity of Charles's barren queen, Portugal was gradually forgotten, and the whole length from the Haymarket to Hyde Park Corner became known by the frivolous name of Piccadilly.

The first to decide to build a house of some size in the unfashionable area of Portugal Street seems to have been Sir John Denham, the absurd, or perhaps tragic, figure who had been given the important post of Surveyor-General by Charles II on the Restoration. Denham in his early years had been a poet of some success, and on the outbreak of the Civil Wars he had thrown himself enthusiastically into the royal cause, with disastrous results to his own side. He was quickly captured and imprisoned, but was later able to assist his royal master, though not in a military sphere. His tenure of the office of Surveyor-General would have been a calamity, since he was quite ignorant of architecture, but he fortunately had the assistance of the brilliant Dr. Christopher Wren. In 1665 the ageing Sir John married a young and pretty wife, who almost immediately became the mistress of the Duke

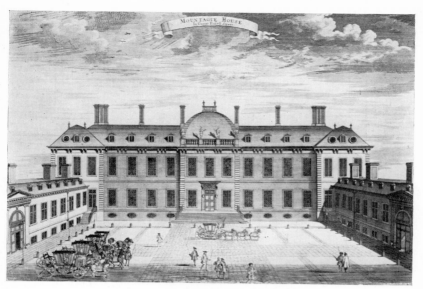

Montagu House, Bloomsbury, as rebuilt in 1687

Montagu House as converted into the British Museum: the great
staircase

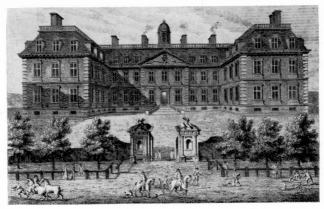

Clarendon House, Piccadilly

Bedford House and Bloomsbury Square: from a painting by Samuel
Scott in the collection of the Duke of Bedford

Bedford House: the entrance front

SEVENTEENTH-CENTURY MANSIONS

of York. Two years later Lady Denham died, poisoned, it was supposed, by her distracted husband. This theory was officially disproved at a post mortem, but a dark cloud of suspicion continued to hang over the unfortunate Sir John, who was for a time out of his mind and died in 1669.

He died, however, not in Piccadilly but at his official residence in Scotland Yard, and it is probable that he never completed his new house, but sold it before his death to the first Earl of Burlington. Richard the Rich, as Lord Burlington was generally known, obtained his immense wealth not from his patrimony, which was modest, but from his marriage with the heiress of the last Earl of Cumberland; he was thus in a position to set up in great style in London. The house which he either built or completed was an attractive brick structure with little ornamentation except for stone quoins and a deep cornice supporting the roof. It was set well back from the road beyond a spacious courtyard, as can still be seen, for the original house is incorporated in the existing fabric. On either side of the courtyard were stables and other outbuildings, each with a subsidiary court of its own; while to the north of the house was a large garden laid out with the rigid formality of topiary and geometrically disposed paths, which was then in fashion. For some description of the interior one inevitably turns to Evelyn, but for once in vain. Though he often met Lord Burlington he makes no mention of his house, and it is probable that there was nothing very lavish or magnificent about the decoration of the rooms: panelling and fine woodwork in all probability, but none of the Continental display which was to be found at Montagu House. Pepys visited Burlington House, but, with his greater interest in people than in architecture, he only remarks on Lady Burlington's admirable qualities, "a very fine speaking lady, and a good woman".

The great social era of Burlington House came under the third earl, the great patron of the arts, who succeeded his father at the age of ten in 1703. This great admirer of the Palladian style did not long leave his house with its homely appearance. As soon as he gained possession of his inheritance the brick façades were concealed behind fine stone elevations with a rusticated ground floor supporting pilasters rising between the first floor windows to a cornice and balustrade. The effect can never have been entirely satisfactory, since the original proportions of the house were hardly suited to this treatment, and now, embosomed in Sydney Smirke's and Messrs. Banks and Barry's heavy-handed rebuildings began in 1867, it looks less happy still.

The most successful of Lord Burlington's alterations to the old house, and one which received universal praise, was an elliptical colonnade which swept round the south side of the courtyard joining the two

"The Man of Taste": Hogarth's famous Cartoon

wings. It was concealed from the road by a high wall, and the sense of surprise which the sudden sight created in the visitor is described by Walpole with his usual vividness. He had been invited to a ball, and had not observed the courtyard on arrival, but "at daybreak, looking out of the window to see the sun rise, I was surprised with the vision of the colonnade which fronted me. It seemed one of those edifices in fairy tales that are raised by genii in a night time." In fact, it would seem to have been raised by Colin Campbell, though the earl, who was only twenty-three at the time, was generally given the credit. The graceful gateway to the court is shown in Hogarth's "Man of Taste", one of those ephemeral satires of which the humour is now dulled. Pope is shown on a scaffolding whitewashing the gateway and at the same time freely bespattering the Duke of Chandos, who has just descended from his carriage, while Burlington bearing a plasterer's hawk climbs an insecure looking ladder. Both in Piccadilly and at Chiswick Villa, which was built about 1730, Lord Burlington exercised a lavish and magnificent hospitality, spending his money freely in support of the arts, particularly of architecture. It is a permanent recognition of his generosity that the Palladian school of architects, which included some of the most talented exponents that this country has ever produced, is commonly known by his name.

On Lord Burlington's death in 1753 his properties passed to his daughter, the Duchess of Devonshire, and during the following century Burlington House was usually let, since the Devonshire family had their own fine house a little farther west along Piccadilly. In 1854 the house was sold to the Government for £140,000. The first intention was to demolish the structure and erect a huge new building to contain the National Gallery, while the Royal Academy would take over the whole of Wilkins' vacated building in Trafalgar Square. The Academy since its foundation in 1768 by Sir Joshua Reynolds had seen much movement. After twelve years in Pall Mall, it had been transferred to Somerset House, where it had remained until 1838, thereafter it was housed in the National Gallery building. After prolonged wrangling covering a decade, the present scheme was finally agreed and work was begun in 1867. The decision to preserve the old house, which, apart from its architectural merits, had so vital a connection with the arts, was exceedingly praiseworthy, particularly at a time when eighteenth-century buildings were not very highly considered, but it cannot be said that the exterior, with its added arcade and ponderous superstructure, seems comfortably placed in its portentous nineteenth-century setting. Some of the original rooms, from one of which Walpole must have gazed out on to the Bernini-like colonnade as it was touched by the first light of dawn, retain to the full their Burlingtonian atmosphere.

Richard the Rich's homely brick house was a modest affair compared to the magnificent pile which Lord Chancellor Clarendon was erecting contemporaneously a little farther along Piccadilly. The situation was a fine one at the top of St. James's Street, looking down on to the Tudor towers of the old Palace lying below it, whence the long slope levelled out into the wooded park. The house, which was begun in 1664 from the designs of the learned and accomplished architect, Roger Pratt, was worthy of the site. The auspices attending its inception, however, were not good, though they were properly indicative of the misfortunes which were to attend its short existence. Two years before the house was begun Charles II had agreed to sell Dunkirk to Louis XIV for five million pounds. This transaction caused violent public outcry, since it was supposed, with considerable justification, that the king was endangering the safety of his country in order to obtain money to squander on his friends; and indeed these thirty pieces of silver must have been a welcome addition to his impoverished exchequer. But though the King was blamed, it was Clarendon who was the principal object of indignation, since it was popularly believed that he had received great financial benefit from the bargain. When he began to build a splendid new house, it was felt that public suspicion was confirmed.

Nevertheless the walls continued to rise with unusual speed, in spite of general hostility, and the design, it was agreed by all *cognoscenti*, was exceedingly pure. The nine-window-wide façade, emphasized by a central pediment, was flanked by deeply projecting wings, and the roof rose steeply above a deep cornice to an extensive flat which was surrounded by a balustrade. In October 1664 Evelyn was taken by the Lord Chancellor and his lady "to see their palace now building", and in the following year Pepys went to visit it and thought it "the finest pile I ever did see in my life". But public animosity to Clarendon increased as the house, which was so unfortunately visible to all, reached completion; while the rumour that the stone of which it was built had been intended for the repair of St. Paul's Cathedral was seized on as a further insult. In August 1667 the Great Seal was taken from the Lord Chancellor, and two months later a bill was passed in the Commons to impeach him for high treason; but it was rejected in the Lords. Nevertheless he prudently left the country, only to return in his coffin for burial in Westminster Abbey in January 1675.

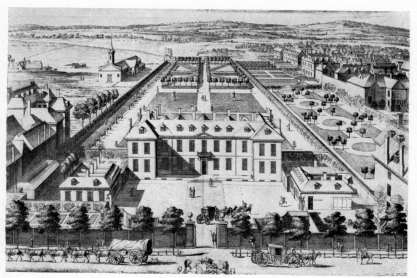

Burlington House

Clarges House

COUNTRY MANSIONS IN PICCADILLY IN THE LATER
SEVENTEENTH CENTURY

Lansdowne House, Berkeley Square

Schomberg House, Pall Mall

Thus he lived for only a few months in the great house which he had built at a cost of over £50,000. On Clarendon's death his son sold the house, which was so closely bound up with his father's misfortunes, to the second Duke of Albemarle for the modest sum of £25,000 with twenty-four acres of land. The Duke, who was the son of the great General Monck and his slatternly wife, known as "Dirty Bess", soon sold it at some profit to Sir Thomas Bond and others. The latter demolished the house, within less than twenty years of its foundation, and laid out on the site the streets of which the names commemorate this transaction. In September 1683 Evelyn walked along Piccadilly "to survey the sad demolition of Clarendon House, that costly and sumptuous palace . . . where I have often been so cheerful and some-times so sad". He goes on to say that it is proposed to build "a most magnificent piazza" on the site, but this ambitious project was rejected in favour of a simple grid of rather narrow, but more profitable, streets.

Few houses of a parallel splendour can have had so short and tragic existence, if one except the first Montagu House, but for one reason or another the great houses of Piccadilly, which were built soon after the Restoration, were all destined to suffer rather adverse fortunes. Berkeley House, lying a few hundred yards to the west of Clarendon, was no exception, though it stood for over sixty years, or more than three times as long as the latter. Its foundation and construction earned no popular opprobrium, for the owner, John Berkeley, had been a courageous supporter of the royal cause during the Civil Wars. In 1658, two years before the Restoration, Charles II conferred on him at Brussels the well merited peerage of Berkeley of Stratton. He must have been a man of affluence, for the house he raised was as splendid as the site on which it stood was large. The area was known as Hay Hill Farm and had a wide frontage to Piccadilly, or Portugal Street, and extended northwards to the boundary of Mary Davies' manor of Ebury. It was an area which was to bring immense wealth to Lord Berkeley's heirs, who possessed the greater part of it until the second quarter of this century.

Immediately on returning to England with his king, Lord Berkeley gave the necessary instructions to Hugh May, who had an official post in the Office of Works and was a talented architect widely employed by those who basked in the sunshine of the restored monarchy. He carried out extensive alterations at Windsor Castle; he made handsome additions to Lord Clarendon's house at Cornbury, which fortunately still stand; he built a moderate sized house for

Sir John Shaw, Eltham Lodge, which was to be the prototype for a great number of kindred buildings in the home counties, which are invariably credited to the inspiration of Wren. Lord Berkeley's choice of architect was therefore a sound one, and it is regrettable that so little is now known of the house which was built at a cost of £30,000.

Clarendon House was several times portrayed; Berkeley was less fortunate, and to form a picture one must principally depend on written descriptions. Evelyn as usual supplies the most illuminating information. The house was in the Palladian style, and the porticoes were copied from one, and the least successful in Evelyn's view, in Palladio's book of architectural drawings, while the planning was apparently not entirely successful. "It is very well built, and has many noble rooms, but they are not very convenient, consisting of but one *Corps de Logis*; they are all rooms of state, without closets. The staircase is of cedar, the furniture princely." The *New View of London* of 1708 describes the pilasters and pediments of the Corinthian order with more enthusiasm, and makes it clear that there were twin pavilions on either side of the entrance court containing on one side the kitchen and laundry, and on the other the stables, both being joined to the main building by curved arcades. Berkeley House was thus an early example of the singularly inconvenient arrangement of setting the kitchen and offices in a flanking pavilion rather than in the main body of the house. The great Palladian houses of the first half of the eighteenth century were almost invariably planned on these lines, with the result that for many years they have presented far greater domestic problems to their owners than Elizabethan or even Tudor buildings. A further reference to the embellishments of the house is to be found in Vertue's notebooks, where he wrote that the staircase was "adorned by the Pencill of Laguerre, the ceiling being an assembly of the Gods of the heavens. The stories on the sides the Rape of Proserpine with ornament and proper decoration."

Lord Berkeley died in 1678, and six years later his widow decided to follow the example of many other owners of great London houses and develop her estate. The house, with a garden of some size, was to be left intact, but the surrounding meadows were to be laid out in streets. Evelyn was called in to advise, which he did with a heavy heart: "I could not but deplore that that sweet place (by far the most noble gardens, courts, accommodations, stately porticos, etc., anywhere about the town) should be so straitened and turned into tenements." His view of the house had clearly mellowed. Clarendon House was already demolished and there seemed little good reason for retaining so large an area of open ground round Berkeley, particularly as Lady Berkeley was to benefit by £1,000 a year from ground rents alone. In spite of this augmentation to the family income, their fortunes for a time dwindled, and early in the eighteenth century the house was occupied by the Duke of Devonshire, who then or soon after bought the freehold of house and garden. In October 1733 the house was burnt to the ground, though much of the contents was saved, and four years later a new Devonshire House, designed by William Kent, began to rise on the site.

One other house stood in this millionaires' row, but though built as a country house it was conceived on more modest lines. This was Clarges House, a high brick building having no architectural pretensions and probably containing the simple panelled rooms which would have been found in any contemporary manor-house. It gains interest from having belonged to Thomas Clarges, the brother of the Duke of Albemarle's sordid wife, who has already been mentioned. Kimber's *Baronetage* of 1771 gives him a glowing descent from John de Glarges, who came to England in the reign of Edward IV. If this were true the family must have suffered a melancholy social decline, for he and his sister were known to be the children of a farrier living in the squalid tenements of the Savoy. He entered the service of the Duke of Albemarle and claimed to have borne the letter inviting his return to Charles II in Holland, and also to have returned with the royal acceptance and a knighthood. The Clarges family were obviously not lacking in the qualities which bring success. He died at Clarges House in 1695, but twenty years previously his son had been created a baronet, and it was the latter who, after considerable trouble with a fraudulent speculator, Thomas Neale, who will be met again in the following chapter, laid out Clarges Street on his Piccadilly property.

Both Berkeley and Clarges enjoyed a pleasing view southwards over the gentle wooded slopes of the royal park towards Westminster and the Palace of Whitehall on the banks of the Thames. Some way down the slope, and just outside the royal precincts, there rose during the first years of the eighteenth century one of the most beautiful of the great houses erected within the purlieus of London. The site, which was originally known as the Mulberry Garden from the trees which had been planted there by order of James I, lay at the end of the long avenue bounding the north side of St. James's Park, while to the west, beyond its own surrounding meadows, the open country stretched away across the marshes of Pimlico to the little village of Chelsea. This pleasant area was bought immediately after the Restoration by Sir Henry Bennett, later Lord Arlington, whose name provided the second "A" in Cabal. Clifford, Ashley, Buckingham, Arlington, Lauderdale have not come down to history as a collection outstanding for probity, but the historian Hume kindly considered Arlington "the least dangerous either by his vices or his talents". In the Mulberry Garden Arlington built a pleasant house of no great architectural pretensions except for a large central cupola, a building barely worthy of its fine position. Some years after his death his daughter and heiress, who had been married to Charles II's illegitimate son, the Duke of Grafton, at the age of four years, sold the place to the Duke of Buckingham. In 1703 Arlington House was demolished and a magnificent new building was begun on the same site. The new owner had no connection with Arlington's colleague in the Cabal, who was a Villiers and had died without issue in 1687. The title of Buckingham had on the whole brought indifferent fortune to its holders—two had been beheaded, one murdered, another had died in a moorland cottage— but it was apparently irresistibly attractive. No sooner had it become extinct in one family than it was recreated for another, and when John Sheffield, Earl of Mulgrave, secured this desirable prize in 1703, there were still claimants living to an earldom of Buckingham. Once again, however, it was not destined to survive, for of the new Duke's three sons only one survived him and he died in Rome of consumption at the age of nineteen. In 1703, however, Sheffield's star was in the ascendant, though he was for a second time a widower and still without an heir. The new house, which was designed by "the learned and ingenious Captain Wynne", as he was called by Colin Campbell, was suitably devised both for its commanding position and also as the habitation of a duke. The large central block was built of brick relieved by stone pilasters and quoins, while the offices were contained in two pavilions lying on either side of the entrance court and joined to the main building by curved arcades. On the frieze of the entrance façade was carved in latin "Thus situated may the household Gods rejoice" and on the garden elevation, with less fertility of invention, simply "Rus in Urbe". The interior was spaciously planned and decorated with the greatest magnificence: walls and ceilings were painted by Gentileschi and Ricci with bold mythological scenes; mantelpieces were of marble, as was the floor of the hall; each of the forty-eight steps of the stair was carved from a single piece of Portland stone; while the handrail was of forged iron. Bas reliefs, niches, and statutes decorated those walls not enlivened with paintings, and Corinthian pilasters framed the Italian artists' rich Olympian groups.

The duke was delighted with his new house and wrote a long letter, which has been preserved, to the Duke of Shrewsbury on the subject. Particularly he liked the position of the house. "The small distance of this place from London, is just enough for recovering my weariness, and recruiting my spirits so as to make me better than before I set out." The view from his garden of the town with its cathedral and palace greatly attracted him, while the garden itself received his careful attention. There were formal avenues of lime trees, carpets of grass, tubs containing bay and orange trees, and a great canal six hundred yards long with groves of trees on either side. From a raised terrace, bounded by a low wall covered with roses and jasmine, a pastoral prospect could be enjoyed of cattle grazing on the rich grass of the meadows. There was much else to charm the eye: parterres and flower gardens, fountains and waterworks, and a kitchen garden "full of the best sorts of fruits". There were a number of greenhouses, in one of which there was "a convenient bathing apartment" which, with the fountains, was supplied from a cistern holding fifty tons in the roof of the house, to which water was lifted by a pump from the Thames. The cost of creating this Elysium is not recorded, but it must have been prodigious, for house and garden as a united composition excelled any of the houses of Bloomsbury or Piccadilly. It was perhaps not quite so large as Clarendon House, but with its spreading wings, courts and gardens it must have surpassed it in beauty and in general grace of composition. A glimpse has survived of the comportment of the Duchess in this great house after the death of her husband and sons. Her life which had been so rich and full had turned to dust, but one comfort remained to her which none could remove while she lived: her royal descent, for she was an illegitimate daughter of James II by Catherine Sedley, Countess of Dorchester. Each year on the anniversary of the execution of her grandfather she gave a melancholy reception at which her guests, who must have grown few with the years, found her seated on a throne-like chair surrounded by her women, all clothed in the deepest sable. It is not surprising that Horace Walpole described her as "more mad with pride than any Mercer's wife in Bedlam".

In 1762 the house was bought by George III from the Duke's illegitimate son, who became the eventual heir, and in 1775 it was settled by Act of Parliament on Queen Charlotte, in exchange for Somerset House. Half a century later it was rebuilt by Nash, though part of the internal disposition survived. Subsequent alterations have given the Palace its present appearance.

Buckingham House was perhaps the last of the post-Restoration London palaces to be conceived with a grand disregard for space such as would be found in a country house set in the midst of a vast estate. Marlborough House, begun in 1709, almost qualifies for inclusion, but the site on which it stands was never of great extent, and the spread of London was already confining the boundaries of its garden. The tide of building was lapping fast over the gardens and meadows of the broad valley in which the town was set: it was a tide which was to develop with the centuries into a mighty flood only to be stemmed by the disasters of the present age.

III

The Migration of Fashion

The eighteen years covered by the Civil Wars and the Commonwealth had brought great changes to the social structure of England. Opulence and power had been enjoyed by a very small class until the fall of Charles I, and these fortunate few had ceaselessly and successfully striven to retain these valuable amenities in their own hands. During the last four decades of the seventeenth century the balance shifted to some degree, and though power was still enjoyed by only a few, wealth became far more widely spread. Many families had been ruined during the Civil Wars, but in general these were the smaller landowners rather than those who had enjoyed vast possessions. The great territorial magnates were still rich, but there were also a large number of merchants who were attaining wealth and importance through commerce, and were to share the distinction and position from which earlier in the century they had been excluded.

The building of huge London houses immediately after the Restoration, which has been described in the last chapter, showed lack of perception of a changing order, and the short duration of the majority is evidence that they were anachronisms almost before the pigments of their painted walls and ceilings had dried. In the country rich landowners could spread themselves as they pleased, but in London it was a different matter: there was a great class of wealthy people clamouring to be housed in a manner befitting their station and in localities which were convenient, but at the same time less crowded and less airless than the City. The population of London was increasing, but, with restrictions on building relaxed, the town was spreading at a greater speed than was merited purely by the swelling numbers. In 1684 Evelyn wrote that London had almost doubled in size "in my time". The diarist was then sixty-four years old and he was referring probably to the growth during the preceding forty years or so, but by far the greater part of this expansion had come in the last twenty-four years: it was during this period that the "mad intemperance" of building, of which he greatly disapproved, had reached its zenith. It is difficult now to assess the rate of increase in population, for though many computations were made, few were based on any calculations which would ensure even moderate accuracy. Chamberlayne in his *Present State of England* suggests that London in 1684 contained over a million inhabitants. If this were true one-fifth of the whole population of England must have been congregated in the metropolis, for Macaulay, who carefully sifted several contemporary and later estimates, reached the conclusion that England contained in 1690 between five million and five and a half million inhabitants. Not only was the birth-rate increasing, but with the less crowded conditions, improved water supply and general hygiene, the death-rate was decreasing. But this was not the only reason for the constant spread of building: the improving roads made the journey to London, even from distant parts of the country, less hazardous and uncomfortable. As a result many county people migrated to London, with their families, servants and carriages, for visits of several months at a time and found it far pleasanter and little more expensive to own a house in one of the new fashionable piazzas or streets, which were rising so fast, than to stay in lodgings. For it was for people of solid financial position, rich squires and prosperous merchants that the new houses were principally designed, for people who wished to live with dignity but without ostentation. The style of house which was being erected during the reigns of the last two Stuart monarchs, with reticent elevations to the street and well finished rooms within, was admirably suited to the way of life of this class.

With the improvement in roads the risks of accident became less, but at the same time the dangers of violent robbery increased. The years on either side of 1700 were the heyday of the highwayman, and rich travellers passing to and fro along the lonely roads provided plentiful and rewarding game. The Flying Coaches, which could accomplish a journey from Oxford or Cambridge to London, for example, in a travelling day of twelve hours, were not particularly vulnerable, but private carriages accompanied by few retainers put up less opposition and at the same time offered richer rewards. Dick Turpin, who owes his aura of romance chiefly to Harrison Ainsworth's fiction, did not begin his squalid career until about 1725 and died on the gibbet at York fourteen years later at the age of thirty-three. By this time the difficulty of making a successful career on the road was becoming constantly greater, and highwaymen must have looked back with regret to the years before 1700, when opposition to their *metier* was very ill organized. In those days it had not been only men such as Turpin, the son of a small Essex innkeeper, who took up this profession, but impoverished members of the upper classes saw here an easy means of earning a livelihood. In the *Verney Memoirs* there are constant references to a reprobate young cousin named Dick Hals who took to this way of life. He spent a few early years in the navy, but soon after the Restoration decided that robbery was more suited to his temperament and talents. He was not particularly successful, for he was twice arrested and on each occasion condemned to death, but escaped "the cart" by the intervention of Sir Ralph Verney and his aunt, Lady Hobart. Once freed he would be invited to spend Christmas with the family at Claydon, and it does not appear that his behaviour was looked on as more than mildly regrettable. However, faults pardonable to youth were less easily tolerated in maturity; and when he was arrested in 1685 his influential relations seemed no longer anxious to secure his release. From his London prison he wrote casually to Sir Ralph, "I have no great news, but only that I think to die next weeke". He was right; a few days later his body was swinging from Tyburn gallows.

Lord Bedford's fine layout on his Covent Garden property has been described in the first chapter. It was a design which was to be emulated in the majority of development schemes carried out during the century following the Restoration, and which, with their spacious residential squares, were to give to London a character enjoyed by no other capital. If it had chanced that some over-all plan had been enforced, such as Wren had devised for the City, a splendid town of long vistas and grand squares would have resulted; but in the event each property was developed individually and without relation to its neighbour, so that no great effect was achieved. The piazza at Covent Garden, begun in 1631, was not only the first square to be built in London, but it was the only one ever constructed in this country surrounded by an arcade. No doubt Inigo Jones had adopted the arrangement from Continental precedents. In 1605, for example, Henry IV of France had decided to build a magnificent square in Paris, principally to provide lodgings for manufacturers of silk, while the spacious arcade below the houses was designed as a public promenade. The Place des Vosges, formerly Place Royale, was the result of this enterprise. A few years later a square of similar design but of even greater dimensions, the Place Ducale, was built in Charville on the Meuse by Duke Charles of Gonzaga; and many French provincial towns followed on a scale suited to their revenues. In Spain, too, though Jones can never have seen them, arcaded squares, where the inhabitants walk in the

51

evenings, are to be found in a number of towns. The finest of these, the Plaza Mayor at Salamanca, was not built until the eighteenth century, but the *plaza* in Madrid was roughly contemporary with the Place des Vosges. Thus London cannot claim to have been a pioneer in laying out spacious squares on symmetrical lines designed for domestic purposes, but at least they were more numerous than in any other city.

In addition to Covent Garden, Inigo Jones made a design dated 1618 for a square of noble proportions on the fields of Lincoln's Inn; but though the square was laid out, only one or two houses were erected, and it was not until 1659, seven years after Jones's death, that building was begun, and then the rigid symmetrical elevations which were originally envisaged were not carried out. This would, indeed, have been difficult to achieve, since a number of people owned small "parcels" of land on the edge of the fields. The area enclosed was, however, of majestic size, and was claimed to be the largest square in Europe, though it has not maintained this eminence. It was also often said that it was of the same dimensions as the base of the great pyramid, but this bore no relation to truth, as it is far larger. Gradually houses rose round the central space. Three early residents, James Cooper, Robert Henley and Francis Finch, received permission to build in 1659 on condition that they conveyed "the residue of the said fields to the Society of Lincoln's Inn for laying the same into walks for common use and benefit". Thus though there was no stipulation on the manner of building, it was made clear that the amenities of the central open space were to be carefully guarded. The residents were men of quality and position who could afford to build houses for themselves of substantial size.

Both Pepys and Evelyn visited Mr. Povey's newly built house in 1664 and were greatly impressed by the beauty of the interior. The former was unusually ecstatic: "And in a word, methinks, for his perspective upon his wall in his garden, and the springs rising up with the perspective in the little closett; his room floored above with woods of several colours, like but above the best cabinet-work I ever saw; his grotto and vault, with his bottles of wine, and a well therein to keep them cool; his furniture of all sorts; his bath at the top of the house, good pictures, and his manner of eating and drinking; do surpass all that ever I did see of one man in all my life."

Evelyn was more succinct, and mentions that the perspectives were painted by Streater, the artist who was shortly to decorate the ceiling of Wren's Sheldonian Theatre at Oxford and to earn the optimistic couplet in Robert Whitall's *Urania*:

> That future ages must confess they owe
> To Streater more than Michael Angelo!

Mr. Povey, who held a number of minor official posts, was a man of taste but not of great distinction: the majority of residents, however, came from the highest class. The Earls of Lindsey inhabited one of the first houses to be built in the square and their name remains attached to it, though they migrated before the end of Charles II's reign to Chelsea; Lord Belasyse, the governor of the Tangier Committee, was here visited in his house by Pepys in 1665; Lord Powis, later Duke of Powis, built himself a particularly fine house in the north-west corner of the square, which still stands under the name of Newcastle House. Lord Powis came to live in the square some time previously to 1681, in which year his house was destroyed by fire, the owner and his family having a narrow escape. Three years later he received permission to rebuild, and the existing dignified brick building arose from the ruins. Though a large house, it has none of the spreading countrified planning of the great houses which were rising, and so swiftly falling, in Piccadilly, and was appropriately designed for its urban position, even going so far as to provide a low arcade for pedestrians beneath its northern side. Powis was a close adherent of James II and suffered considerably in his cause. Twice his house in Lincoln's Inn Fields was attacked and narrowly escaped destruction, but he was eventually rewarded with a dukedom, one of the few peerages created by James after he had lost his throne. Lord and Lady Powis left England with the King and died at St. Germain. In the following century the house was acquired by Thomas Pelham Holles, Duke of Newcastle-upon-Tyne, that rather engaging politician who was apt to dissolve in tears on the slightest cause. He died in the house in 1768. A resident in the Fields of less illustrious origin, but one whose name has remained fresher than that of these noble politicians, was Nell Gwynne, who for several years lived in the square under the disapproving eye of her neighbours. These were her affluent years when she was supported by the King, her Charles the Third, as she called him: her First was Charles Hart, the great-nephew of Shakespeare, her Second Charles Sackville, later Earl of Dorset, and finally there came her royal lover. In 1670 her eldest son by the King was born in her house and christened Charles Beauclerk. At the age of six he was created Earl of Burford and a

53

few years later Duke of St. Albans. His mother, unlike other the royal mistresses, received no title, though it is said that the King had intended to create her Countess of Greenwich and was only prevented by his sudden death.

Though the houses rising round the square were of considerable magnificence and the residents were in general people of substance and position, the large central area, which had been so carefully preserved as an open space, retained its bucolic character to an unwelcome degree. Here was thrown refuse from the surrounding streets and houses, while amongst the bosky undergrowth great numbers of beggars and vagrants found convenient cover. As soon as the coach of one of the noble residents was seen, a flock of importuning scoundrels would crowd round in so determined a fashion that progress was often impossible until largesse had been distributed. At night a striking change would come over this squalid throng; the piteous cripple of daytime would develop unexpected strength and agility with the sinking of the sun, and there was great risk in crossing the square after dark. Gay in *Trivia* puts the disagreeable situation into pleasant verse:

> Where Lincoln's Inn's wide space is railed around,
> Cross not with venturous step; there oft is found
> The lurking thief, who, while the daylight shone,
> Made the walls echo with his begging tone.
> That crutch, which late compassion mov'd, shall wound
> Thy bleeding head, and fell thee to the ground.

The rails mentioned by Gay were no more than wooden posts marking the division between the roadway and the timbered central space. It was not until the reign of George II, after the Master of the Rolls, Sir Joseph Jekyll, had been attacked and nearly killed in the square, that it was decided properly to fence this dangerous area and to lay out a garden. Within this fence, "an iron pallisade fixed upon a stone plinth" a garden was created on symmetrical lines with a large central basin and radiating paths between lawns, an arrangement which has now given way to a more informal design. In addition to the unattractive company lurking amongst the bushes of the square, there was another factor which may have detracted slightly from the pleasant residential character of the Fields: it was occasionally used as a place of execution. During the reign of Queen Elizabeth some of the band of fourteen youths, headed by Anthony Babington, who

Newcastle House, Lincoln's Inn Fields

Fashion in Grosvenor Square

Poverty at Seven Dials

VICTORIAN LONDON

conspired to restore Mary Queen of Scots to liberty, had been hung and disembowelled on a scaffold in these then open pastures; and this perhaps created a precedent for holding the execution of William Lord Russell in this fashionable square during July 1683. Possibly it was intended that the sad spectacle of so prominent a nobleman's unhappy predicament would have chastening effects behind the dignified façades which looked out on to the scaffold. Lord Russell met his death with the courage usually shown by sufferers on these occasions. He was accompanied to the scaffold by Doctors Burnet and Tillotson, the former of whom wrote an account of the melancholy proceedings: "He prayed by himself, then Tillotson prayed with him. After that he prayed again by himself, then undressed himself, and laid his head on the block without the least change of countenance; and it was cut off at two strokes." Russell's conviction of high treason seems to have had little justification, and his connection with the Rye House Plot was not with certainty established.

Building was spreading fast over the meadows to the north and west of Lincoln's Inn. A short way to the west in the Parish of St. Giles the enterprising, the rather excessively enterprising, Mr. Thomas Neale was laying out a considerable area on a plan of his own. The site was roughly rectangular; in the centre he formed a circular space from which seven streets radiated to the outer edge of his property. As a focal point for his star of streets he raised a Doric pillar with a sundial facing the opening of each street. The layout was of sufficient interest for Evelyn to inspect and to describe in his diary, but though the idea was sound, it was conceived on mean lines, and Seven Dials can never have been impressive. The rate books for this area have disappeared, but it would seem that it never attracted the fashionable world, as its owner doubtless hoped, and it became rather a colony of French *emigrés* who flocked to this country after the Revocation of the Edict of Nantes in 1685.

Neale was one of the many irresponsible Restoration characters who found money easy to make, and easier to lose, in the carefree atmosphere of the Court. He is said to have lost two fortunes before he was made Master of the Mint and Groom Porter to the King; the latter post he held also under William III. For the former office he received a salary of £500 a year, but for the latter, which cannot have been very onerous, a modest £2 13s. 4d. with his board in addition. This income provided a steady background to his building speculations, which he organized by means of public lotteries. This was a usual means of financing these operations and was still favoured almost ninety years later, when the Adam brothers were endeavouring to build at a profit in the Adelphi. It must have offered an attractive speculation, an elegant new house in Seven Dials for a £10 ticket. His project, however, was not a success, and his agreement to purchase Clarges House and its meadows, described in the last chapter, led him into further financial difficulties; at his death about 1699 he was insolvent. Early in his career he had attempted to secure some easy money by making a prudent marriage to a rich widow, suitably named Lady Gold. There were several other suitors in the field and the widow's family were determined to prevent the marriage to Neale, but the widow apparently was keen, and Pepys describes how it was achieved: "She called Neale up to her, and sent for a priest, married presently, and went to bed, . . . and so all is past." Thus the marriage was celebrated and consummated before intervention was possible. Lady Gold probably later regretted her impetuosity.

Thomas Neale did not embark on his Seven Dials speculation until towards the end of Charles II's reign: a few years earlier in 1672 a lease of the meadows on the west had been granted to the Earl of St. Albans, who had no connection with the subsequent dukes, with permission to build. The ground had been the property of the Queen Dowager, who died in 1669, and seems to have been once again in the possession of the Crown by 1677, when Charles granted it to his son the Duke of Monmouth. It was a convenient manner of providing for one of his expensive brood. After the duke's attainder and execution James II returned it to his widow, who held it for a few years, and later William III gave it to his young compatriot William Bentinck, Earl of Portland. How these royal meadows came to have the name So Ho, sometimes spelt with an "e" after each "o", remains unsolved but as early as 1632 the name is found in the rate books of the parish of St. Martin's. It is said that "Soho" was used by Monmouth's supporters as the watchword of the day at the battle of Sedgemoor. It brought them little good fortune.

The duke was twenty-nine when he received the grant of Soho fields, and the layout, which had probably been already begun, proceeded swiftly. A great square was formed in the middle of the area named, with becoming filial duty, King's Square; to the north a short straight street connected it to the Oxford highway, to east and west similar streets led respectively to the road to Charing village and Whitehall, and to other long cross streets set out on the property. Two streets led from the south side of the square and between these, set back from the road behind an iron grill, stood Monmouth House, its tall, rather menacing façade looking northward over the square.

Monmouth House, Soho Square

Wren's name is inevitably connected with the design of the house, but this great man would never have perpetuated so freakish an elevation, which seems, with its curious Jacobean detail and widespread broken pediment, to have been rather the work of a man barely conversant with classical principles. The history of the house was neither long nor happy. After the duke's execution it was sold to the Bateman family, but as the social centre of London moved westward it was abandoned as a private house, and after an interlude as an auction room, it was demolished towards the end of the eighteenth century. Meanwhile the royal connection with the square seemed best forgotten and it was renamed Soho Square.

A century earlier, however, the prospects for the new building estate were exceedingly rosy. The Duke's mansion gave glamour to the neighbourhood, and the spacious, well-built houses which arose in the square and in the neighbouring streets were soon inhabited by families of the highest position and fortune. The mistakes of Lincoln's Inn Fields were carefully avoided and the central space was firmly enclosed by an iron paling and the area within neatly laid out with paths and lawns, in the centre of which a statue of Charles II rose from a circular stone-rimmed basin. Into this pool water gushed from four figures, carved by Caius Gabriel Cibber, representing the great rivers of England.

Although the façades of the houses were not designed as a single composition, the elevations were all so similar, with three floors above a basement and an attic in the roof, which rose from a deep wooden cornice, that an effect of complete unity was achieved. Each house was entered through a pilastered and pedimented doorway, sometimes placed centrally with two or three windows on either hand or set on one side with anything from two to four windows flanking it. The placing of the entrance indicates fairly certainly the planning which would be found behind these reserved façades, for there was a little variety in the sane straightforward arrangement of the houses of this period. The front door would open into a spacious hall, stone paved with perhaps black Purbeck marble squares let into the junction of the stones. An easy stair, in oak or cedar with delicately carved balusters, would climb up three sides of the hall arriving at a gallery on the first floor. It would have been rare that the walls would be painted as beautifully as at 75 Dean Street, where Hogarth had expended his genius to bring beauty to the house of his father-in-law, Sir James Thornhill; perhaps also he was prompted by a spirit of rivalry to show that he was able, in the delicacy and gaiety of his scenes, to surpass the great master himself. In some houses the stairs would be in stone with a handrail supported on uprights of forged iron. At first floor level the grand staircase would stop and the journey upwards could be continued

The original layout of St. James's Square

Soho Square about 1800

Hanover Square

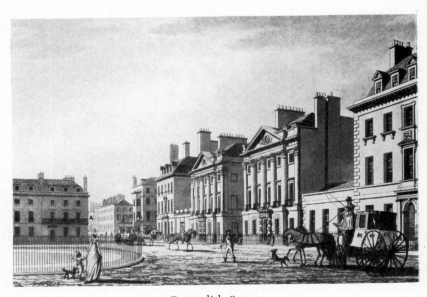

Cavendish Square

EIGHTEENTH–CENTURY SQUARES

on a modest stair set beyond the hall and extending from basement to attics. One one side, or both if the house were double-fronted, would be agreeable rectangular rooms with one or two more of very similar proportions at the back looking on to a small garden, for most of these Soho houses had space for a lawn and a few trees, a fig or a mulberry. On the first floor the plan would be similar, but perhaps with the area of two rooms thrown into one. Here the large-scale panelling which lined all the rooms would be more elaborately finished: the carving of detail on the architraves, doors, shutters, chair-rails, indeed on every moulding, would be richer and more delicate; while, before the century was out, there would certainly be a few carved wooden swags of an exquisite lightness surrounding a picture on the chimney breast cut by that incomparable genius Grinling Gibbons.

The furniture in these late Stuart houses was rich but sparse. The wide oak or elm boards of the floors would be covered by no more than a small central island of carpet, against the wall might be an oriental cabinet, one of the products of expanding trade to the Far East, set on an elaborate gilded stand of English workmanship. There would be a commode inlaid with woods of various colours and ivory, perhaps stained to a vivid green; a table supported on legs with luxuriant curves; and a few chairs with high carved backs. Silver sconces on the walls and a few candles on the tables would provide a fitful illumination, though occasionally a wooden chandelier, carved and gilded, spread a soft brilliance through the room. The most elaborate features of Stuart furnishing were the majestic four-poster beds. The beds of the Elizabethans were robust affairs with short, heavily carved posts supporting a ponderous canopy. As ceilings became higher so likewise did the beds, and those designed for the lofty Carolean and William and Mary bedrooms were of a portentous height. The canopies, which were made of wood, were carved with all manner of scrolls and mouldings of classical form and then covered with material, often crimson velvet or brocade. The head boards were treated in a similar style and often included the initials of the owner or the coronet of his rank. The summits of these majestic creations were ornamented with urns or *panaches* of feathers. The bedrooms of the average Stuart London house, such as those in Soho Square, were not constructed on a scale suitable for beds of this size. The reception rooms of the ground and first floor might reach a height of twelve feet or so, the latter being rather higher than the former, but the first bedroom floor was seldom more than ten feet high. Thus these great beds were usually destined for country houses or for the decreasing few London houses able to accommodate them.

During the third quarter of the seventeenth century a system of postage was evolved, and it became increasingly important to adopt some easy means of identifying houses. The very large houses, as we have seen, were usually called by the title of the owner if he were a peer; but few commoners gave their houses their family name. Thus the addresses on letters became very complex and must sorely have puzzled postmen, who were anyhow barely able to read. Lady Sussex addressed a letter to Sir Ralph Verney "Att his hose in Lincolnes Inn fields in the middle of the Row where the Spanish Embassidor lies", and in 1676 a letter was addressed a little more exactly to the same house "Next dore to the Black Balcony in Lincolln's-Inn Fields in Holburne Row". The address which Lady Hobart gave of her new house was "A greate house in Chancery Lane, near the Three Cranes, next dor to the Hole in the Wall". Shops usually had names and were indicated by signs in the same way as inns, so that they were more easily distinguished, but a predominantly commercial thorough-fare, such as the Strand became, must have presented a bewildering spectacle. There seems to be no record of who first had the happy notion of giving numbers to houses, but with the building of several new squares and many long streets, it must have been essential to find some means of lessening the confusion and giving assistance to the employees of the Post Office.

The Post was fairly well organized in 1687, when Chamberlayne compiled his *Present State of England*. From London "letters and pacquets" were dispatched on Tuesdays, Thursdays and Saturdays to all parts of Great Britain, and on the other three weekdays to the Continent. A single sheet of paper could be sent eighty miles for twopence and two sheets for twice that sum; while by means of the newly introduced penny-post a letter or parcel up to a pound in weight and £10 in value could be sent for a modest copper anywhere within a radius of ten miles of the City. Chamberlayne reckoned that a reply to a letter from three hundred miles away would be received in five days. In view of the difficulties of transport, this system, if indeed it worked as well as Chamberlayne contends, must have been remarkably efficient. More than a century and a half was to pass before Rowland Hill was able to write in his diary: "Rose at 8 h. 20 m. Penny Postage extended to the whole Kingdom this day."

For more than a century Soho retained its position as a centre of elegance and fashion, and for half a century longer Soho Square could boast an atmosphere of solid residential respectability. Richard Payne Knight, the rich Hereford squire who was a devotee of the picturesque in landscape and in art, had a house here until his death in 1824. Four years earlier death had removed the most learned resident the square had ever had, Sir Joseph Banks. Here, behind the elegant eighteenth-century façade of his house in the south-west corner, were kept his collections of insects, fishes and plants, and also his library of immense value, all of which are now in the English museums. The Duke of Argyll, the first Earl of Berkeley, Lady Fauconberg, Oliver Cromwell's third daughter, and many others of note were residents. The first Earl of Macclesfield, who was tried and convicted of mal-practices during his long tenure of the office of Lord Chancellor, died here in 1732, and Alderman Beckford, vastly rich, twice Lord Mayor of London and father of the eccentric William Beckford of Fonthill, lived here during the middle years of the eighteenth century.

It was in a *cul-de-sac* close to Soho Square that Dickens placed the quiet lodgings of Doctor Manette in the *Tale of Two Cities*, when he settled in London after his years of captivity in Paris. The Doctor and his daughter, Lucie, inhabited two floors on each of which were three large rooms, while the invaluable Miss Pross had charge of the kitchen in the basement. In the courtyard at the back stood a large plane tree in the cool shade of which the Doctor and his friends would sit on summer afternoons. When Dickens was writing Soho had already greatly altered since the last decade of the eighteenth century, when his "Tale" was enacted; now, almost a century later, it has changed more drastically still.

The majority of the residents of Soho were people of substance, remembered for their high birth, political importance or intellectual qualities: a very different figure, and one who survives merely as a flamboyant, social character of a rather dubious variety was Mrs. Cornelys. In 1760 she took a lease of Carlisle House—not the attractive brick house in the street of that name, but a large house on the east side of the square where St. Patrick's Roman Catholic church now stands. Both these houses had been built by members of the Howard family, the former by the first, the latter by the third Earl of Carlisle. The building, with its spacious reception rooms and general air of distinction, was admirably suited to her enterprise, which was to organize fashionable parties and routs on a basis financially rewarding to herself. For a woman of her dubious background this would have seemed a difficult achievement, but probably little was known of her origin. In fact, she was born in Venice in 1723; at the age of seventeen she became the mistress of a senator, and thirteen years later of the Margrave of Beyreuth; in addition she made a few appearances in opera and was twice married. From these varied sources she had amassed sufficient money to set up at Carlisle House in great style, but it must have been her attractive personality which enabled her to persuade people of the highest rank to become members of her society. In this she was completely successful. In the winter of 1760 discreet notices appeared in the *Public Advertiser*: "The Nobility and Gentry, Subscribers to the Society in Soho Square, are acquainted that the Third Meeting is on Thursday next . . . to begin at seven o'clock." The Soho Assemblies room became a social institution and for a decade Mrs. Cornelys' revels became increasingly brilliant. They are mentioned by Smollet in *Humphry Clinker*, where Lydia Melford writes ecstatically to Laetitia Willis: "I have been at Mrs. Cornelys' assembly, which, for the rooms, the company, the dresses, and decorations, surpasses all description." The masked ball in February 1771 was the climax of her success; the company included two royal dukes and innumerable members of the peerage. Unfortunately a discordant note was introduced into this fashionable gaiety. As in Prince Prospero's fête in Poe's *Masque of the Red Death* a sinister figure appeared with the face of a corpse peering through the folds of a white shroud and carrying a coffin. This grim reminder of mortality seems to have thrown a chill on the distinguished company; likewise it marked the beginning of Mrs. Cornelys' decline in fortune. Shortly after, she appeared at Bow Street accused of keeping a disorderly house and was fined £50. Her patrons quickly deserted her, and in 1772 the magnificent contents of her "Temple of Festivity" were sold by auction. She made several attempts during the following years to restart her assemblies, but with little success, and in 1795 she made a last bid to attract the fashionable world by setting up in Knightsbridge as a "Vendor of Asses' Milk". This wholesome beverage, however, did not attract the popular taste, and she was soon in the Fleet Prison, where she died in 1797.

Simultaneously with Soho, the area immediately to the south-west was being developed. The central square, Golden Square, was as spacious as King's Square, but the streets surrounding it were meanly laid out and the district never achieved the fashionable *cachet* of Soho. Furthermore there was a small field in this area possessing a sinister reputation. Here had been the great pit into which the bodies of those who had died of plague were thrown. Each night carts carrying their terrible load of fresh victims came to the field and cast their burden into this communal grave. For many years it was supposed that the ground was infected and that there would be danger to life if it were disturbed, so that this little field was left as a malignant oasis amidst the buildings which rose round it. Gradually the corrupting bodies were forgotten and the tide of building eventually swept over the Stuart skeletons without harm to the living. Nevertheless Golden Square, which seems to have been called after its builder, could boast some distinguished residents: Lord Bolingbroke lived here, when not at his country house at Battersea, and Hatton in the reign of Queen Anne describes it as "a very new and pleasant square". But the poor layout of the district always mitigated against its residential popularity, and Pennant's remark that the square was "of dirty access" expressed the situation very concisely. Angelica Kauffmann lived in the square from 1767 until she left England fourteen years later, and here she made her unfortunate marriage to the bogus Count de Horn; but the square was already losing its popularity and the little streets were occupied by tenants of a very different sort from those the original builders had intended. The fashionable world was again on the move partly north-ward but principally westward.

Southampton, later Bloomsbury, Square, the inauguration of which was described in the last chapter, retained its atmosphere of aristocratic respectability all through the eighteenth century. The ducal house occupying the north side gave a tone to the neighbourhood which Soho could never emulate once it had been invaded by Mrs. Cornelys' raffish assemblies. Architecturally these two squares had much in com-mon: the houses were spacious and handsome, reticent without, but admirably appointed within, and in many cases splendidly furnished. Into this fine square, so redolent of dignity and security, there burst on the night of 7th June, 1780, a violent, menacing mob. The Gordon Riots had broken out and the house of Lord Mansfield, the Lord Chancellor, in the north-east corner of the square, was the principal objective of the murderous throng. The entrance door was soon broken down, the mob rushed in and hurled the contents of the house, includ-ing the precious manuscripts and library of books into the street where they were heaped on to a great pyre and burnt. Meanwhile the Lord Chancellor and his wife, whose lives would have been in danger if they had been found, escaped by a back door. With the demolition of

Bedford House the square lost a little of its aristocratic flavour, and with the turn of the century it was prosperous business men and those of moderate means rather than leaders of politics or fashion who were to be found as residents. Isaac D'Israeli, the father of Benjamin, who came to live in the square in the first years of the century, was representative of the new, but still highly respectable, order. A little way to the east Red Lion Square, which we have seen Dr. Barbon laying out in the 1680's, followed a roughly similar course, though the small houses never attracted people of such consequence as those in Bloomsbury. That there were still aristocratic residents there at the end of the eighteenth century we learn from Leigh Hunt, who as a small boy was taken by his parents to visit "an old lady of quality" in 1790. The incident would have passed from his mind but for the fact that in the course of polite conversation the old lady's false teeth fell out. This little social catastrophe made a lasting impression on the boy.

Soho and Bloomsbury were fine squares, but even more ambitious was the square and adjacent streets built on the royal meadows near St. James's Palace. From Fairthorne and Newcourt's map of London, which was drawn in 1658, it can be seen that the rectangle of fields sloping up northwards to what is now Piccadilly was as clear of buildings as the fields farther west, where is now the Green Park, indeed more so, for there was one building, Berkshire House, with a spacious garden, in the south-east corner of the latter. Charles II, who found it difficult to reward in a material manner those who had deserved well of him, must have welcomed the opportunity for granting a lease of forty-five acres to the same friend who, as we have seen, held for a few years the lease of Soho Fields, Henry Jermyn, Earl of St. Albans. The general form of the layout contemplated by Lord St. Albans was very similar to those of Covent Garden, Soho and Bloomsbury. Here also there was to be a magnificent central square, in which it was hoped the houses would eclipse in grandeur those already existing at Covent Garden and Lincoln's Inn Fields; while the streets round the square were to contain houses of smaller but still very adequate size. It was particularly and reasonably supposed that the proximity of the district to Whitehall and St. James's Palaces would make it attractive to those whose duty or pleasure lay at the Court. But a difficulty arose in that these rich noblemen were unwilling to build houses of the importance and size contemplated on leasehold sites; and it thus seemed that the grant of the land, which had appeared to hold such agreeable financial possibilities, was to become an onerous liability for Lord St. Albans.

The awkward situation, however, was resolved by the indulgent monarch, who, in answer to a humble appeal converted the leasehold into a freehold; thus Lord St. Albans was able to proceed with confidence. During the sombre year of the Plague the work was brought to a standstill, but the Great Fire of the following year provided a violent stimulus to building, and it appears from the rate books that within a year or two the houses in the surrounding streets, King Street, Jermyn Street and Charles Street, were completed and inhabited. In the great square covering over six acres building operations proceeded more slowly, for the houses were constructed singly by the purchaser of a plot, though the vendor was able to stipulate that there should only be built "palaces fit for the dwellings of noblemen and persons of quality". The social and architectural standards of the square were thus to be kept on the highest possible level.

The first house to be built, suitably enough, was St. Albans House in the south-east corner of the square; whence his Lordship could conveniently supervise the progress of his speculation. Later, when his prosperity increased, he moved across to the north side of the square at the western corner of York Street, where his house had a frontage of one hundred and twenty feet, as compared to the sixty-five of his first home. The elevations of the houses as they rose adhered to an overall plan. There was no attempt, as was usually done in later squares, to form each side into a composition, but all the houses simply conformed in design, so that each side of the square resembled somewhat a range of Wren's Chelsea Hospital. Each house had three stories of tall windows and a uniting cornice ran along each range from which a steep-pitched roof rose broken by dormer windows. About a century later, when it would seem that many of the houses had become structurally unsound, they were demolished piecemeal and re-erected to any design favoured by the owner.

With the great influx of population to this area it was necessary to provide for their spiritual needs. St. James's Fields had been part of St. Martin's parish; they were now detached, and Sir Christopher Wren designed a handsome church to stand at the end of York Street with its principal entrance in the centre of the south side so that the pillared and pedimented doorway formed a suitable climax to the view up the street. When the north side facing Piccadilly became the principal elevation the entrance was moved. Work on St. James's Church was begun in 1682 and finished a few years later. Meanwhile the gaps in the square were filling up most satisfactorily and the houses were occupied by families of the highest quality. Lord Belasyse moved from Lincoln's Inn Fields to a large house adjacent to St. Albans House; Lord Arlington, who, as we have seen, owned a house on the edge of St. James's Park, bought a large site on the north side of Charles Street; but the house was inhabited by his brother, Sir John Bennet. In the north-east corner the energetic builder Dr. Barbon was building a house for the Earl of Kent, while two doors away on the north side another speculative builder, whose works were principally confined to Westminster, Abraham Storey, was carrying out a similar work for John Hervey, uncle of the Earl of Bristol. John Hervey mentions the house in a codicil dated 1677: "Since the making of my last will I have purchased of Mr. Abraham Story a capitall messuage with the appurtenances scituate on the north side of St. James Square." This and the contents he bequeathed to his wife for life and then to his heirs. He died in 1679, but it was not until December 1698 that Lord Bristol wrote in his diary: "Dear wife with ye whole family removed from Jermyn Street to my house in St. James Square." Shortly after, he insured it for £5,000 for seven years, paying a premium of £75 at "ye Rainbow Coffee house . . . in ffleet Street". And on 1st November, 1714, the twenty-sixth anniversary of his marriage, he noted proudly: "His Majesty King George did me ye honour to supp with me at my house in St. James's Square." It was no doubt a gratifying attention, but a tedious evening.

Other early residents were the Earl of Oxford, Lord Purbeck, Lord Halifax, and Arabella Churchill, the future Duke of Marlborough's sister. Though the morals and behaviour of some of these may have been rather questionable, Lord St. Albans was at least able to congratulate himself that his splendid new square, which was more or less completed by 1680, was inhabited by people of the highest class. There was, however, one most regrettable intrusion. In the last house in the square, the site of which is now covered by the Army & Navy Club, there had come to live the notorious actress and singer Moll Davis, who was one of the king's mistresses. She had apparently first attracted the monarch's attention by her singing of "My Lodging is on the cold ground". The pathos of her song so moved the emotional royal heart that she was without delay given a house in the grandest square in the town.

The principal rooms of these houses were arranged to look out on to the square, but most of the sites were so planned that there was space for a small garden at the rear. None of these was large, but those on the east side, where St. Albans had built his own first house, were more advantageously placed than the remainder. Unfortunately the central square did not at first present an agreeable aspect. Before the fields were developed a fair had for many years been held in them. St. Albans, in the interests of his venture, reduced the fair to the status of a market, and this, with the unavoidable attendant squalor, took place in the square. Nothing is more contagious than rubbish: seeing refuse already left in the square, people from the poorer districts came and added their own. It became, as Macaulay described it, "A receptacle for all the offal and cinders, for all the dead cats and dead dogs of Westminster." This unsavoury condition must have greatly mitigated against the pleasure of living in this distinguished neighbourhood, but nevertheless it was not until 1726 that an Act of Parliament was passed enabling the freeholders to enclose the square, and the market was set up at a discreet distance from this fashionable neighbourhood. The first layout of the square was rather austere. An octagonal area was enclosed by iron railings at each corner of which was a stone pillar nine feet high and surmounted by a lamp. Within this barrier was a large circular basin one hundred and fifty feet in diameter and over six feet deep, to which water was supplied by the York Building Company. The majority of the houses, on the other hand, received a supply of water from the New River Company. This ornamental pool had the dual purpose of forming an elegant feature and also a reserve of water in the event of fire. Some years earlier than this a legacy had been left by one Samuel Travers for the erection of an "equestrian statue in brass to the glorious memory of my master King William the Third". The project seems to have aroused no enthusiasm amongst the noble residents, and it was not until 1806 that the bequest was remembered and the figure by Bacon, which now caracoles so gracefully beneath the plane trees, was set up.

It was not to be expected that a square inhabited by such wealthy freeholders would for long maintain its original appearance. With changing owners and changing taste in architecture there seems to have been constant rebuilding in progress throughout the eighteenth century: larger houses were demolished and two or three smaller ones built on the site, or the reverse took place and one large house was raised on the area of two smaller ones. The latter was the case with Lord St. Albans' first house, which with part of Lord Belasyse's original freehold adjacent made way for Norfolk House, designed by Matthew Brettingham about the middle of the century. The house had had many

67

owners since St. Albans left it, and it had been much enlarged by the first Duke of Portland, who built additional rooms on the court at the back. It was in a room of this back wing, which survived Brettingham's later reconstruction, that George III was born on 4th June, 1738, less than ten months after his sister, later Duchess of Brunswick. Frederick Prince of Wales rented the house on being turned out of St. James's Palace by his irate father, and remained there for some years before moving with his family to Leicester House. A description of the old house has survived in a letter written by Lady Wentworth about 1708 which gives very accurately the aspect of a late Stuart house. "It has three large rooms forward," she wrote, "and two little ons backward, closetts and marble chimney-peicis, and harths to al the best rooms and iron backs to the chimneys. Thear is twoe petty clossets with chimneys and glas over them, and pictures in the wenscoat over most of the chimneys." All this would have seemed very old fashioned by the middle of the eighteenth century, when William Kent and the Palladian architects had developed the taste for decoration of great magnificence. Brettingham's elevation to the square, in yellow brick with stone trimmings, was restrained, even severe, but the fine rooms of the interior were as rich and elaborate with carving, gilding and mirrors as the consummate craftsmen of the period could make them.

Where so much first-class domestic architecture was concentrated only a few examples can be mentioned. In the north-east corner the house of the Earl, later Duke, of Kent was destroyed by fire soon after 1720 and is said to have been rebuilt from the designs of Lord Burlington. The great saloon on the first floor overlooking the square, modelled it would seem on the Double Cube Room at Wilton, was, and fortunately still is in spite of nineteenth-century adornments, one of the grandest rooms in London. Across the square Athenian Stuart provided an example of the rather empty purity of his Greek revival architecture in a pillared and pedimented façade; but the most beautiful building in the square, a masterpiece of design and planning, is number 20, which Robert Adam built for Sir Watkin Williams-Wynn in 1772. The frontage of the site was not broad, only forty-five feet, but the depth was considerable, and Adam gave full play to the brilliant ingenuity of his planning so as to provide a sequence of spacious and varied rooms giving the effect of a house designed without restriction of site. It is probably one of the most successful houses ever built in London, and its future, though not as a private house, seems most fortunately assured. So much history has passed in St. James's Square during its three centuries of existence, so much fine architecture has existed there, and some still does, that it is difficult to move away. It is perhaps some of the less important incidents in its history which strike the imagination most forcibly: the Duke of Hamilton's body being carried back in his coach to his house, and to his unsuspecting widow, after his fatal duel with the profligate Lord Mohun; the grand display of fireworks to celebrate the peace of Ryswick said to have cost the huge sum of £10,000; Queen Caroline's daily procession during her trial from the square to the House of Lords through a throng so dense that her string of carriages could barely pass. No other residential square can claim so high a place in the history of London and one must be thankful that its air of distinction has not quite left it yet.

Pall Mall and St. James's Street, which bound the area, are two of the oldest roads in the metropolis, having been thoroughfares to St. James's Palace long before there was any building along their verges. The former, with the open fields to the north and the royal park to the south, was for long a favourite walk of Londoners, and it did not lose its popularity when buildings began to enclose it. Pepys constantly refers to walks in "the Pell Mell" with his colleagues and friends at a time when houses must have been fast rising. Residentially the south side of the street was the more attractive, since the backs of the houses faced pleasantly southward over the park. One of the finest of these houses was Schomberg House, of which three parts still stand. It is sometimes said to have been built during the Commonwealth, but Fairthorne's map of 1658 shows not a single building between a cluster of houses at Charing, now roughly Cockspur Street, and St. James's Palace. In any case the style, showing strong Dutch influence, places it fairly certainly in the reign of William III and the tradition that it was designed by that singularly fertile genius Daniel Marot is not improbable. It must have been a dignified structure, with its red-brick walls and stone dressings, before it suffered such cruel mutilation in 1850. The first Duke of Schomberg, who gave the house the name which it has retained, came to England with William III and became second-in-command of the army. He was killed at the battle of the Boyne. The third duke, with whom the title became extinct in 1719, greatly embellished the house and commissioned Peter Berchett to paint landscapes in lunettes on the staircase. Some years after the Duke's death the house was sold by his son-in-law and was eventually acquired by the portrait painter John Astley. It was less his artistic accomplishments than a prudent marriage with an opulent widow which provided the funds for the purchase of so large a house, and he put the building to good use by sub-letting part of it to Gainsborough, who came to live there when he left Bath in 1774, and remained there until his death from cancer in the throat fourteen years later. Much of Gainsborough's finest work was carried out during his residence in Pall Mall. A few doors westward of the Duke's splendid home was the elegant little house given by Charles II to Nell Gwynne, who moved here from Lincoln's Inn Fields after the birth of her royal bastard. The neat and modest elevation of the building gave no clue to the luxury of the interior. A plain pedimented doorway with a single window on either side gave ingress to the house and a simple pediment topped the narrow two-storied façade. Mistress Gwynne's taste in decoration must have been rather flamboyant, and there is a tradition that one of the rooms was panelled throughout, even to the ceiling, with mirror, though it remains a little uncertain whether it was in fact Nell or Moll Davis, in the house across the street at the corner of St. James's Square, who adopted this narcissine style. In any case it must have been unusual at this period, though it was repeated by a number of ladies of a kindred vocation during the following centuries. The house stood until the third quarter of the nineteenth century, and, a repentant Magdalen, purged the loose ways of its early life by spending its last years as the home of the Society for the Propagation of the Gospel.

Pall Mall and St. James's Street have now developed into thoroughfares of a very similar character, but in the seventeenth century, when houses were first rising along their borders, the former was entirely residential, and residential on rather a high plane, while the latter from the first was partly commercial, and the houses, of which there were a considerable number, were primarily lodging-houses. The private houses were not on the grand scale: they were rather of the modest size, such as Sir Christopher Wren owned. To St. James's Street he used to drive from his house at Hampton Court to carry out his work as superintendent of the fabric of Westminster Abbey, the only official post left to him during his last years. In the course of a drive to London in February 1723 the nonagenarian architect caught a chill, and died in his St. James's Street house a few days later. The famous residents of the street have been legion, but almost all lived in lodgings. The poet Waller lived on the west side for seventeen years until his death; Pope had rooms here for many years; over Elmsley's bookshop Gibbon died in 1794. Gilray had rooms on the east side and here he committed suicide in 1815 by throwing himself from the window. About the

Leicester Square in 1753 and 1874

Holland House

Bridgewater House

LONDON MANSIONS: JACOBEAN AND VICTORIAN

same time Byron occupied lodgings towards the bottom of the street. Amongst the shops and lodging-houses stood the coffee-houses which soon blossomed into the clubs, which still line these streets, though the fine classical buildings date from the eighteenth and nineteenth centuries. Thus St. James's Street may be said to have retained its character, from the residential angle, since its inception more than two and a half centuries ago. In the reign of William III the street was given up to shops, lodging-houses and coffee-houses; now in the reign of George VI it is still consecrated to shops, flats and clubs, with the addition of offices. No street in London can have maintained its character for so long. But its architectural aspect has greatly changed. Only three little houses on the east side survive to show how the street must have looked. It was bordered by simple three-storied houses, the ground floor set level with the street so that the whole building was kept low, while between them ran the impressive thoroughfare, as broad and straight as one of Le Notre's great canals, with the unimpressive buildings of the royal palace at the foot and Lord Chancellor Clarendon's sumptuous house at the top.

Southward across St. James's Park the tide of building was lapping the royal domain as closely as it was on the north. There was no layout or buildings comparable to the scale and dignity of St. James's Square, but a number of narrow streets were built across the swampy meadows lying within the purlieus of the Abbey and the broad spaces of Tothill Fields. In 1660 there were only scattered houses along the narrow thoroughfares which must have been little more than lanes; forty years later houses were close built over the area lying immediately south of the park and were stretching more loosely towards the walls surrounding the large garden of Peterborough House, near the banks of the river. The houses in general were small and designed in the simple, comfortable style of the decades on either side of 1700. Their modest proportions and sane planning have led to their survival, for their plainly panelled rooms are as well suited to the life of today as they were to that of two and a half centuries ago. Close to the park, however, the houses were more ambitious. The narrow street running roughly parallel to the edge of the park broadened out at one point into a small square which was called Queen's Square, later Queen Anne's Square, to differentiate it from various others of the same name, and eventually, in the middle of the last century, with the addition of adjacent Park Street, Queen Anne's Gate. The majority of the houses on the park side have been rebuilt, but those on the south side of the square are as good an example of a range of late Stuart houses as is to be found in London. Though the elevations form no composition, as they would have done if built later in the century, they conform to a single design with string courses, window levels, cornices carried through the whole range. A group of buildings designed on these lines could be extended indefinitely. With their discreet use of ornament in the keystones to the windows, the finely carved canopies to the entrances, and their general air of comfort, they represent perhaps the most attractive style of English domestic architecture for medium-sized houses.

These houses of Park Street and Queen's Square with their view into the park were the homes of many famous men, but there is one character who one associates with this street more clearly than any other since he was portrayed by Zoffany in the setting of his home. In the picture painted about 1782 Charles Townley is shown seated in his library in Park Street with three friends. The room is high, top lit and quite plain except for a narrow cornice and a marble chimney-piece of the style favoured by Robert Adam. Though the decoration is so simple the contents are exceedingly elaborate, for here are gathered together Townley's great collection of Greco-Roman marbles. Every object of his collection, it would seem, has been introduced into the picture so that only a small space is left in the middle of the room for a few folio volumes left negligently open on the floor and for a dog sleeping at his master's feet. The collection was very highly considered and after Townley's death was purchased by the British Museum for £20,000; today, a century and a half later, the majority of the marbles are of little value.

Westminster during the first decades of its development was not a residential quarter of fashion but rather of convenience, owing to its proximity to the Palace of Westminster. The social world, or that part of it which could not afford the scale of St. James's, was more inclined to move to the new areas bordering the north side of Piccadilly. As has been described in the previous chapter, Lady Berkeley was negotiating the leasing for development of the fields round Berkeley House in 1684, but it was not until ten or twelve years later that the principal feature of the area, Berkeley Square, was built, though the streets running back from Piccadilly along the garden walls were begun earlier. The south end of this long rectangle covering five acres was not at first built up, the area probably forming an extension of Berkeley House garden, but in 1760 or 61 this agreeable site was bought by the then Prime Minister, Lord Bute, who at once began building a large house from the designs of Robert Adam. The experience of Lord Clarendon a little less than a century earlier might have been a warning of the dangers of an important member of the government housing himself with undue magnificence. Perhaps Lord Bute thought his position secure. If so he was mistaken, for the populace did not fail to connect the signing of the unpopular Peace of Paris in February 1763 with the sudden rise to affluence of a Prime Minister who had been known to be far from wealthy. Whether popular outcry was too much for him or his means were less ample than he had supposed, he decided to part with his unfinished house. The sale presented no difficulties since he had been successful in buying the site from under the very nose of Lord Shelburne, who was equally desirous of building a house in this attractive position. Shelburne, later Marquis of Lansdowne, was delighted with his good fortune, continued building on the original design with a few modifications, and came to live in the house in August 1768. Lady Shelburne showed rather tempered enthusiasm. "It is very noble," she wrote in her diary, "and I am very much pleased with it, tho' perhaps few people wou'd have come to live in it in so unfinished a state." However her lord wished it and she obediently acquiesced. Noble the house was, indeed, rising grey and dignified beyond a wide expanse of lawn bordered by plane trees, with the air of a house in the country. In his planning Robert Adam as usual showed his resource, for the house though spacious was compact, and the side pavilions, which in a country-house would have lain at the end of long curved arcades were here tucked close to the main body. The building in its present altered guise gives little indication of its original charm.

Unlike the majority of squares laid out towards the end of the seventeenth century, Berkeley was not built to a single unified design. Each leaseholder constructed his house according to his taste, but as could be seen from the large number which survived until the 'thirties of this century, the effect was remarkably united and harmonious. No square in London had more character and charm, and this was greatly enhanced by the gnarled plane trees, planted about 1789, which still stand in the central garden, and by the gentle slope on which it is built. Buckley Square, Thackeray named it in *Yellowplush Papers*, and many other authors have set the scenes of their romances in the dignified houses. Until the demolition of the east side, the square retained the residential character it had possessed since it was built, but perhaps the second half of the eighteenth century saw the climax of its elegance. In 1779 Horace Walpole moved into a house on the east side from Arlington Street. "I came to town this morning," he wrote to Lady Ossory, "to take possession (of my house) in Berkeley Square, and am as well pleased with my new habitation as I can be with anything at present." He died in the house in 1797. Five years before Horace Walpole came to the square, Lord Clive had committed suicide in his large stone-faced house on the opposite side. He had left India with an immense fortune in 1767, but the anxiety and worry of the parliamentary enquiries into his actions had unhinged his mind. He was only forty-eight when he died. A few doors from Lord Clive's house is a building of moderate size designed by William Kent, which almost rivals Robert Adam's house in St. James's Square as a masterpiece of town-house planning. Kent's house is about forty years the earlier of the two, and covers a much smaller area, but by subtle planning he introduced a room of great size and splendour on the first floor with a high coffered ceiling which absorbs the space of the second story. The staircase also is contrived with extraordinary ingenuity. The elevation to the square is well proportioned but plain, and shows that air of reserve which the majority of Palladian architects preferred to present to the outer world.

It was a house on the same side, No. 50, now occupied by Messrs. Maggs, which was for many years reputed to be so haunted as to be almost uninhabitable. This grim rumour seems to have started soon after the middle of the nineteenth century, when, for one reason or another, the house remained untenanted for many decades. Why it should have been empty for so long has never been satisfactorily explained, It was said to have been rented by several families who hastily left within a few days of their arrival; or alternatively that it belonged to an eccentric old man who came to the house only once or twice a year and, though never staying in it, declined to give it up. Almost inevitably it was suggested that coiners were busy at their nefarious trade behind the murky windows and crumbling façade, and the fact that the position of the house would have been a conspicuous one in which to carry on this industry was apparently no impediment to the story. As to the ghosts themselves, there were a number of different versions. There was said to be the figure of a child, who had been starved to death in an upper room; the wraith of a young woman who had thrown herself from a window in order to escape the attentions of her uncle. There was said to be a phenomenon so terrible in one of the rooms that those who saw it sometimes died of the shock and those who survived would never speak of it. Sometimes, when the house was completely empty, sounds could be heard of heavy furniture or cases being dragged across the bare floors, and bells would ring loudly. The sinister tradition lingered, but was never explained. Now, however, that the house has abandoned its residential career for that of commerce it would seem that the ghosts and wraiths have obligingly departed.

The great financial success which attended the development of the Berkeley property encouraged Sir Richard Grosvenor, the fourth baronet, to embark on a similar scheme in the northern part of his manor of Ebury about 1695. The open fields extending north-west from Berkeley Square to Tyburn covered almost a hundred acres and had been inherited by Sir Richard from his mother, Mary Davies. At the time of Mary Davies' marriage in 1677 to Sir Thomas Grosvenor she was considered an eligible heiress, but the meadows of Ebury Farm, extending from Knightsbridge to the Thames with the hundred acres to the north, were of much less value than the rich Cheshire lands of her husband. The apparently inexhaustible demand for new houses for the rich soon reversed this position, and since 1700 Mary Davies' meadows have never ceased to increase in value. In deciding the layout of the new building estate, Sir Richard adopted the conventional arrangement: a great square of six acres was placed in the centre of the estate and around it a grid of streets was planned. No attempt was made to form a common line or axis with the Berkeley estate and the junction of the two was completely haphazard. The garden in the square is said to have been laid out by Kent and was surrounded with "palisado pales placed upon a circular dwarf wall", in the centre Sir Richard set a gilt equestrian statue of George I. As in Berkeley Square, the houses conformed to no uniform style. Each leaseholder built as he felt inclined with only a few restrictions such as the alignment of the façades and the height of the buildings; the elevations could be in brick or stone, or of brick with stone trimmings. Whatever the design or material each house represented a complete composition and nowhere were several houses joined to form a single architectural unit.

One of the earliest residents in this new and elegant square was Ermengarde Melusina von Der Schulenberg, perhaps the most important of George I's many mistresses. She and Countess von Platen arrived in England in the train of the Hanoverian monarch and within a few years were rewarded with the English titles respectively of Duchess of Kendal and Countess of Darlington. The people of England were accustomed to royal mistresses, and that they should be highly rapacious was accepted as inevitable, but at least they were expected to be attractive. In this respect George I's mature matrons fell far short of Stuart precedent, for one was far too thin and the other far too fat. Thus they gained the nicknames of the "Maypole" and the "Elephant and Castle": it was the former who graced Grosvenor Square with her presence. Her elder daughter by the king married in 1733 the famous Lord Chesterfield, and the large fortune which this daughter inherited on her mother's death ten years later, though only secured after rather squalid haggling, enabled Lord Chesterfield to build a magnificent house in South Audley Street, one of the streets laid out by Sir Richard Grosvenor on the grid plan round his splendid new square. It was in Grosvenor Square that the Cato Street Conspiracy was designed to fructify. On the evening of 23rd February, 1820, the Cabinet Ministers had arranged to meet at Lord Harrowby's house for dinner. The crazy plan of the conspirators was to break into the house during the meal, murder as many as possible of the distinguished guests, then, with the enthusiastic support of the populace, which they confidently anticipated, seize several buildings of importance in the metropolis. The project, however, was given away by one of their number and the conspirators were apprehended. Four were executed and the remainder sent as a useful contribution to the meagre population of Australia.

The hazardous custom of selling a house by means of a raffle or lottery was occasionally resorted to throughout the eighteenth century. In 1739 the fine centre house on the east side of Grosvenor Square was disposed of in this way. The value of the property held on a long lease at £42 a year was assessed at £10,000, but there is no record as to the sum raised by the sale of tickets. It is to be hoped that the transaction was more favourable to the vendor than that of Sir Ashton Lever's museum at Leicester House, Leicester Square, in 1784. In this case Sir Ashton proposed to sell forty thousand tickets at one guinea each. In the event only eight thousand were sold, but the vendor took twenty-eight thousand himself and allowed the raffle to proceed. It proved an unlucky gamble, and the museum passed into the hands of an obscure man who had laid out only two guineas.

The Grosvenor estate in Mayfair achieved the highest social status from its inception. The houses in the square were the larger, but those in the adjacent streets had an elegance which only now, as the area loses at last its residential character after more than two and a half centuries, is beginning to fade. The streets laid out on the west side of Berkeley Square, Curzon Street, Charles Street and Hill Street shared an equal and sustained popularity in the fashionable world. Before the middle of the eighteenth century the "blue-stocking" Mrs. Montagu was established in a house in Hill Street where, an assiduous follower if not a leader of fashion, she decorated a room in the Chinese taste. "The Empire of China" she called her house, but the desired effect was not achieved without considerable trouble. Linnell, a competent designer of furniture in the classical style, was invited to turn his talents to the oriental manner, but at first with only moderate success. "If Mr. Linnell designs to gild the bird he sent me the drawing of," she wrote with asperity, "it will look like the sign of the eagle at a Laceman's door. If japanned in proper colours, it will resemble a bird only in colour, for in shape it is as like an horse." When Mrs. Montagu later moved to Portman Square, as will be described in the next chapter, these oriental fripperies were abandoned for the Grecian taste. In this same street at the beginning of the nineteenth century Sir John Leicester, later Lord de Tabley, kept his fine collection of pictures in a large gallery built out at the back of his house. It was about the same date, apparently 1820, that Becky Sharp and Rawdon Crawley came to live in Curzon Street, having cunningly eluded their creditors in Paris. It was a discreet and well-chosen locality for an adventuress and her complaisant husband; and it was also fortunate that the former butler of the Crawley family, Mr. Raffles, should have sunk his savings in the purchase of this little house and its contents. Thus the young couple easily found a suitable place in which to practise the art, so fully described by Thackeray, of living on nothing a year. Poor Mr. Raffles ended in the Fleet Prison, but for Becky a more glamorous career was in store.

IV

Georgian Development

It might have been expected that the spate of building which was inaugurated during the reigns of last Stuart monarchs would have more than absorbed the demands of the families of wealth who were in search of accommodation: but it was not so. The houses in the wide areas of St. James's and Mayfair were built and occupied at a steady rate; and squares and streets which during the first years after their layout had been bordered by isolated houses, before the death of Queen Anne presented a continuous built up frontage.

The western stretches of the Tyburn road had formed something of a dam against the tide of Stuart development, but early in the reign of George I the waters burst their temporary bounds and swept northward on to the property of Edward Harley, Earl of Oxford. In 1713 the earl had made an advantageous marriage with the heiress of John Holles, Duke of Newcastle. Of this lady Swift wrote to Stella: "the girl is handsome, and has good sense, but red hair". She had also about half a million in money and vast estates at Welbeck, Wimpole and on the edge of the rapidly expanding metropolis. It was these latter, which lay along the northern side of Tyburn road, which were so clearly destined for profitable development. In 1718 Cavendish Square, named after the countess' grandfather, was laid out a few hundred yards to the north of the highway and from it the usual geometrically planned network of streets was devised stretching away into the open fields to the north and west. All the new streets were given names derived from family or territorial connections.

The planning of the new estate was not quite on the grand scale of the Grosvenor property; Cavendish Square was barely half the size of its rival across the Tyburn road, and the streets were a little narrower, but it was designed to attract the noble and the rich, and succeeded in so doing. Several houses of great size were built in the square; there was Harcourt House on the west side and the mansion of Lord Bingley, one of the fortunate directors of the South Sea Company, on another, and Lord Foley's fine house was only a little way out of the square. Lord Bingley's house was later inhabited by the

The Buckingham House of Queen Anne's Reign

The Buckingham Palace of Queen Victoria

Belgrave Square

Fitzroy Square

Hertford House in Manchester Square

second Duke of Portland, who had married Lord Oxford's only child and heiress. On the north side of the square the great Duke of Chandos, perhaps the most extravagant builder in an age of extravagant building, contemplated a huge mansion. The project was never carried out, probably owing to the involved condition of his finances, and later the existing pair of Palladian buildings, each containing two houses, was erected on the site. The central garden, on to which these fine houses looked, was badly maintained. Dodesley writing in the middle of the eighteenth century mentions its neglected condition disparagingly: the surrounding rails and wall were much decayed "and make but an indifferent appearance".

It seems probable that Lord Oxford's venture was not proving as financially rewarding as he had anticipated, and that, temporarily at least, saturation point for large houses had nearly been reached. Certainly his own affairs had become exceedingly involved in spite of the wealth brought by his marriage. Four-fifths of his wife's fortune had disappeared by 1740 owing to his "indolence, good nature and want of worldly wisdom", and the situation was not fully remedied by the sale of the Wimpole estate for £100,000. As many unsuccessful speculators before him, he endeavoured to drown his cares, and at the age of fifty-two he died. His incomparable library was sold by his widow, the collection of manuscripts going, as has been seen, to the nation and forming part of the nucleus of the British Museum.

When Cavendish Square was planned the district directly to the south of it across the highway to Tyburn was still open, but by 1720 Hanover Square had taken its place, at least in outline, on the maps of London. In area the square approximates to Cavendish, but it contained fewer houses of great size, with the exception of Harewood House, which stood until this century on the north side. Charles Knight in his history of London says that from the list of original occupants it appears that almost all were generals. In an age when the foremost soldier in the country could be given a palace such as Blenheim and vast sums of money as well, it would seem that a military career was more financially rewarding than now.

The generals of Hanover Square must certainly have been gentlemen of means. A few of the original houses remain to show their spacious design and fine finish. Many must have resembled number 3 Tenterden Street, a few doors from the square, which retains almost unaltered the dignified air which was so strong a characteristic of early Georgian architecture. Robust railings in forged iron stand before the tall red-brick façade, four windows wide and now reduced in colour to the common London denominator. The entrance opens, as was usual, directly into a stone-flagged, two-storied hall, up the walls of which climbs to a first-floor gallery a stone stair with an iron balustrade. A secondary stair, concealed from the front part of the house, rises from basement to attic, while the principal rooms open from hall and gallery. This house is in no way unusual, except that it has had the good fortune to survive. The scale is moderate, but no planning could give a greater sense of space or be better adapted to the needs of a social life. It was probably to a house such as this "in a street not far from Hanover Square" that Tom Jones accompanied after a rout a masked woman who turned out to be Lady Bellaston, an encounter which led to the fortunate young man finding himself possessed of a much-needed £50 note in the morning. The very spaciousness of the planning of houses of this type has led to their destruction, since when mere office space is required fine halls and well proportioned rooms are uneconomic, and double the floor area can be obtained on a similar ground space by means of low ceilings and narrow staircases.

It was in George Street, now canonized, that Lady Mary Wortley Montagu came to live in 1761 on her final return to England after twenty-two years abroad. This once brilliant figure had sadly altered in the intervening years: she was suffering from an incurable disease which was to allow her only a year to live, her appearance was entirely neglected, and if Horace Walpole's account of her is true, her character had sadly deteriorated. "I think her avarice, her dirt, and her vivacity, are all increased," he wrote. "Her dress, like her language, is a galimatias of several countries: the ground-work rags, and the embroidery nastiness." The description was not designed to evoke any feeling of pity: nevertheless it can hardly fail to do so.

Hanover Square was not able fully to maintain its first promise of social or military elegance, and as usual, as the inhabitants lost a little of their distinction, the general aspect of the place began to decline. The author of *Critical Observations on the Buildings and Improvements of London* presents a dark picture of the appearance of the central square in 1771: "It is neither open nor enclosed. Every convenience is railed out, and every nuisance railed in. Carriages have a narrow, ill paved street to turn in, and the middle has the air of a cow yard." Nevertheless with Lord Harewood on one side of the square, Lord Palmerston, the father of the Premier, on the other and the gallant Lord Rodney also a resident, the fashionable flavour was not quite lost, though the presence of the rather rakish assembly rooms run by Gallini was inclined to lower the aristocratic tone.

The Oxford enterprise was not the first project for development in the fields to the north of the highway. A little to the west an ambitious scheme had been contemplated during the reign of Queen Anne for a large square, which was to have been called after the Queen and to have had a church in the middle, as in Smith Square in Westminster. The plan, however, fell through and the area remained an open field until a lease was bought from the Portman family by the Duke of Manchester as a site for his London house. The place attracted him, it was said, owing to the proximity of duck shooting in the country to the north, though it would hardly have seemed very propitious for this sport. The house was begun in 1776, a plain structure in brick and stone with Corinthian pilasters supporting a cornice and balustrade. South of his house was laid out a square, but houses rose only slowly round it and it was not fully built up until the last decade of the century. Though of little architectural importance Manchester House was destined to survive where many houses of far greater distinction have been ruthlessly demolished; and, as the Wallace Collection, its future would seem to be as assured as any London building. The house was barely completed when the Duke died, and his heirs sold it as a residence for the Spanish Ambassador. Close by was the Catholic chapel attached to the Embassy, and this, later, led to the building of St. James's Spanish Place. It was to this chapel that Charlotte Brontë went during her visit to London in 1851, and not unexpectedly she viewed it with unfavourable Protestant eyes. "On Sunday," she wrote, "I went to the Spanish Ambassador's chapel, where Cardinal Wiseman, in his archiepiscopal robes and mitre, held a confirmation. The whole scene was impiously theatrical."

Manchester House, however, was no longer the Spanish Embassy: for a time the French Ambassador lived there and later it was acquired by the second Marquess of Hertford, whose wife was so close a friend of the Prince-Regent. It was his son, the third Marquess, who began to form the collection which was to become one of the most famous and valuable in the world. His marriage to Maria Fagnani had brought him great fortune, since both the Duke of Queensberry and George Selwyn were pleased to consider this daughter of the famous Marchesa Fagnani their child, and both left her a fortune. The Marquis of Steyne and Gaunt House were modelled on Lord Hertford and the splendours of his home; but the fluttering Lady Steyne was no prototype for the dazzling Maria. Disraeli also introduces him into *Coningsby* as Lord Monmouth, a nobleman of not very amiable character and belonging to "a family famous for its hatreds". But as an art collector he was outstanding, and the fortune of two millions he left at his death in 1842 was a testimony to his business capacity. It was Lord Hertford's son, the fourth Marquess, who left the collection, which he had greatly augmented during his life, to his illegitimate son Sir Richard Wallace, whose widow bequeathed it to the nation in 1897; three years later the house was opened to the public.

As the eighteenth century advanced both landlords and speculative builders became more cautious: the abandonment of the Queen Anne's Square scheme, the financial difficulties of Lord Oxford were both indicative of changed conditions. The happy years following the Restoration, when rich clients were competing hotly for frontages in each new area as it was laid out, were over, but still a constant though less urgent demand continued. A gentle pressure westwards was maintained throughout the century: the City was abandoned residentially by all but a few; Covent Garden had changed its character; Seven Dials with some of the smaller streets of Soho were inhabited by people who could not possibly be considered as belonging to the world of fashion.

Large additional building operations on the Bloomsbury estate and on adjacent areas during the latter part of the century were to absorb, as will be described shortly, large numbers of families of what would now be called the middle income group; but those who considered themselves as belonging to the cream of social life and to whom expense was not of first importance turned their eyes still farther westward. The great Grosvenor estate had filled up without great delay, the Oxford estate had slowly reached completion, it must therefore have seemed to Henry Portman that his two hundred acres of farm land at Marylebone on the north side of the Tyburn turnpike were fairly ripe for development during the opening years of George III's reign. In 1764, then, a great square, roughly equal in size to Grosvenor Square, was laid out and named by the owner after his own family, as was usual. The work was carried out by a speculative contractor of the name of Abraham Adams. Since these great squares were not at this time given any unity of elevation there was only one point to decide in planning them, once the main lines had been settled: should the streets enter the square at the centre of each side or in the corners? Precedent gave no clear indication. In Inigo Jones' design for the Piazza at Covent Garden the former was the arrangement, as also in

Portland Place

Adelphi Terrace

BUILDING DEVELOPMENTS OF THE ADAM BROTHERS

Lower Regent Street, looking towards Carlton House

The original Regent Street Quadrant

Soho Square on three sides; Cavendish and Hanover presented a compromise; in Grosvenor two streets enter close to each corner, but leaving a fairly substantial block between their junctions with the square. In Portman the street openings are kept closer to the corners, but one was left open to provide space for a house of some magnitude, a description of which will shortly be given. There were advantages in both sorts of layout: the central axis would have been effective where the central area was open and where, as practically never occurred, one square led to another laid out on a similar plan; on the other hand it removed the possibility of building a central house in each range of larger and more dominant character than its neighbours, which was the usual convention when no set elevations were enforced.

In Portman Square the builders of houses were given licence to build as they pleased, and though the frontages varied in width there was no attempt to set a "master" house in the centre of each side. As it happened by far the largest and finest house built in the square, with the exception of Mrs. Montagu's "isolated villa", was near the north-west corner and fortunately still stands. The Countess of Home, for whom it was designed by Robert Adam, was the vastly rich and child-less widow of the eighth earl. Her fortune came, as did many at that period, such as those of the Lascelles and Beckford families, from the West Indies. Her magnificent house was begun exactly a decade after the square was laid out and was finished four years later. In Home House Adam had a simpler problem than at Sir Watkyn Williams-Wynn's house in St. James's Square, since, with a wide frontage allowing a breadth of five windows, he was able to plan the house almost as a square. As was usual with Robert Adam, the planning is masterly and infinitely resourceful: no two rooms are alike either in decoration or in form, and recesses, niches, columns are introduced to break up the rectangular shapes into ever fresh variety.

It is curious that Robert Adam, whose talent for planning for beauty of effect was prodigious, should seldom have considered such a practical detail as easy access from kitchen to dining-room. In most of his houses "the Eating Room" was so placed that food would have to be carried across an entrance hall or past the main stair, and often it would enter the dining-room by the same door as the guests. In hygiene, however, he was greatly in advance of contemporary archi-tects. The majority of his large London houses was provided with a w.c. on each of the principal floors, usually constructed with a window for ventilation and opening out of a boudoir or dressing-room at the back of the house. At Home House, exceptionally, this convenience was omitted, unless windowless cupboards in the middle of the two main stories were designed for this purpose.

Building in the square progressed slowly, and houses, once built, were not easily disposed of. James Wyatt, whose architectural practice was second only to that of the Adam brothers, bought the leases of several sites at the east end of the north range and raised houses on them as a speculative venture. He seems eventually to have disposed of them fairly profitably, but the process was neither quick nor easy.

Lady Home may have lived in the most beautiful house in the square, but the queen of the whole neighbourhood was indubitably Mrs. Montagu. In 1775 she had been left a widow with a large fortune and extensive estates and coal mines in Yorkshire. After a few years of travel she returned to London, took a lease of a large site at the northwest corner of Portman Square and commissioned James Stuart to build a house of a suitable size to accommodate the large, but highly intellectual, assemblies she proposed to give. Stuart's style of architecture, founded on close study of the buildings of ancient Greece, represented an advance on the frivolity of the Chinoiserie manner of which she had been a devotee a few years earlier; but what it gained in purity it decisively lost in gaiety, and the fine house which he erected had little of the lightness and beauty which the more eclectic manner of Robert Adam, for example, bestowed on buildings. However, Mrs. Montagu managed to introduce an element of fantasy of her own contriving into the cold Grecian rooms: the Cupidon room was painted, according to Mrs. Delany, with wreaths of roses and jessamine amongst which gambolled plump cupids; in the Feather Room the hangings were made exclusively of the plumage of exotic birds. Both these rooms must have caused the architect some pain and surprise. It was on the theme of the latter room that Cowper wrote a poem beginning:

> The birds put off their every hue
> To dress a room for Montagu;
> The peacock sends his heavenly dyes,
> His rainbows and his starry eyes
> The pheasant, plumes which round infold
> His mantling neck with downy gold.

By 1781 Mrs. Montagu was happily settled into her new house and her social activities continued on a grand scale to within a few years of her death in 1800. The ardent hostess is a target for spiteful criticism in all ages, but Mrs. Montagu must have had much beyond her money to attract the intellectual world to her parties for so long a period, some quality of character beyond mere zest for entertaining. Her own mental abilities were said to have been of an unusually high order, and her letters show that she had command of a graceful literary style, but it cannot be said that they now provide much interest or amusement. One of her particular charities was her May Day dinner for the young chimney-sweeps of London, which took place in the garden in front of the house, when they were plentifully regaled with roast beef and plum pudding. The house remained the home of the builder's collateral descendants until 1874, when the lease reverted to the Portman estate, and it then became the home of Lord Portman. Now nothing but the crumbling walls of this once famous house rise amongst the weeds and brambles of what was once a garden.

The success which the Adam brothers achieved with their London houses probably prompted them to embark on some speculative building on their own account. A site of unusual possibilities and in a highly convenient district was, as it happened, available. In Chapter II it has been described how Durham Yard, lying on the slope between the Strand and the river, had been built up in the seventeenth century with small, ill-constructed tenements which were only fit for demolition a century after their erection. This was the site of which the Adam brothers obtained a ninety-nine year lease in 1768 at an annual rent of £1,200. Unfortunately the noble owner, the Duke of St. Albans, being confined for debt in Brussels, benefited little from the transaction. The scheme which the Adam brothers devised was to construct a huge foundation containing cellars, vaults and wharfs near the river bank, and thus to form a great platform on a level with the Strand on which the grand terrace overlooking the water, with several adjoining streets, could be built. It was a bold and expensive project, and entailed hazards of a nature which no other speculative builder had encountered in laying out streets on flat or gently undulating ground. But the risk seemed to the brothers justified in order to provide the houses on the terrace with one of the most beautiful and extensive prospects to be obtained anywhere within the metropolis.

Unfortunately the enterprise begun with such high hopes and enthusiasm was destined to bring nothing but trouble and financial loss to the brothers. Many unexpected difficulties arose: the river bank had to be extended outwards to overcome the trouble of stinking mud which was uncovered at low tide, the huge bastion, rising forty feet above the river, proved immensely costly to construct, the vaults within it were often flooded and so impossible to let profitably; while the houses themselves, in spite of their superb position, elegant design and decoration, and ingenious planning, were unaccountably slow in finding purchasers. The drawback to the houses on the Royal Terrace, as it was called, was the narrowness of their frontages compared to their depth, thus the rooms were inclined to be long and rather dark, while the provision of a double basement, even in times when the welfare of servants was little considered, may have been thought inconvenient. In 1773 the brothers decided to resolve their difficulties by inaugurating a grand lottery with the opportunity of drawing a house for £50. By this means their most pressing difficulties were alleviated. Before the lottery it seems that only three houses in the terrace were occupied, one by the builders themselves, the next by David Garrick and a third by Dr. Graham.

To Mr. and Mrs. Garrick's house came all the intelligentsia of London: their entertainments had none of the formal nature of Mrs. Montagu's routs, but were achieved with a lack of trouble and expense which she may well have envied. Amongst the throngs of visitors appeared on one occasion the unlikely figure of Jean Jaques Rousseau. During his short and melancholy sojourn in this country he was taken by Mrs. Garrick to the theatre to see her husband acting, and since it was known that Rousseau was to be present and public interest in him was great, the place was crowded. Rousseau enjoyed the play immensely though understanding barely a word of English, but Mrs. Garrick spent an anxious evening, for, as she told Joseph Craddock, "the recluse philosopher was so very anxious to display himself, and hung so forward over the front of the box, that I was obliged to hold him by the skirt of his coat, that he might not fall over into the pit". After the performance he was taken to the Adelphi for "an elegant supper" at which the "first literary characters" were invited to assist. It does not seem that Mrs. Montagu was ever able to persuade this Continental lion to her house.

Garrick as a resident was a great asset to the Adelphi. Dr. Graham's presence, though people flocked to his house, was a rather doubtful advertisement, for the house was known as "The Temple of Health", and his methods of advertising his theories were eccentric and the treatments prescribed exceedingly expensive. The leaflets which were handed out proclaimed "The Celestial Brilliancy of the Medico-

Electrical Apparatus in all the Apartments of the Temple". The clinic had no more than a temporary success and the doctor himself eventually died in a lunatic asylum.

The houses of the terrace were the first since the building of the Covent Garden Piazza more than a century earlier to be united into a single architectural composition. The original houses in St. James's Square had had uniformity, but there was no attempt to give their elevations any architectural grouping. Robert Adam was thus the first, with this single exception, to introduce the system of composite building, which most subsequent urban architects were to adopt with great exterior effect, but in many cases with diastrous results on internal planning. The design of Adelphi Terrace, until mangled by additional decoration in the nineteenth century, was extremely reticent and consisted of no more than pilasters on the central and end projections supporting a frieze and cornice. It demonstrated clearly the ability of the brothers to deal successfully with a long range of houses, and it was not surprising that in 1774 they were commissioned to devise a scheme for a street of rather special grandeur on the eastern side of the Portland estate. From the already existing Foley House a wide road was to lead northward towards the wooded fields of the Crown property which stretched away towards the Hampstead hills. On either side of Portland Place, as it was to be named, were to be isolated houses of great size so that it would become a street of palaces which would rival the great avenues of the Continental capitals. Designs and plans for houses for the Earls of Kerry and Findlater were drawn out in detail by Robert Adam, while James Adam, who apparently was seldom allowed to perpetuate an independent design, produced a handsome scheme for a great range to take up much of the west side of the Place. The ambitious plan for the avenue of great mansions fell through, and the scale of the houses in James's range was found to be too large for any demand, but a restricted scheme, principally the work of the latter, was eventually arrived at, and until demolition and destruction were brought to work, made Portland Place as fine and dignified a street as any in London.

Robert Adam's only other ranges of houses in London show a different spirit. Until well past the middle of the eighteenth century the area lying between the Oxford, Portland estate and Tottenham Court Road remained open fields. A short road, Rathbone Place, ran from Oxford Street up to a windmill and reservoir which, amongst other uses, supplied water to the basin in Soho Square; beyond to the north were meadows containing several ponds, and forming part of the Manor of Tottenham, which belonged to the second Duke of Grafton, the grandson of Charles II. Across these meadows at right angles to Tottenham Court Road a fine new thoroughfare was constructed which after many years as the "New" Road was named the Euston Road after the estate of the Dukes of Grafton in Suffolk.

The proposal to build a new road from Islington to Paddington on the Edgeware Road had first been mooted in 1755, but had encountered fierce opposition from residents in Bloomsbury, who conceived that it would destroy the amenities of their quiet squares and streets. The line of the road lay well to the north of the Bedford estate, but nevertheless the Duke was prevailed upon to make a strong protest on the grounds that the dust raised by traffic would have a deleterious effect on his fields. The Duke of Grafton, who foresaw a great commercial improvement to his estate from a new highway, was in the opposite, and eventually victorious camp.

As the latter duke had expected, once the New Road was completed his sequestered meadows became prospective building land, and in 1790 he commissioned Robert Adam to lay out Fitzroy Square on the south side of the road. In the event only the south and east ranges were built from Adam's designs, the remaining two following some time later when the international situation was less unsettled. The designs were almost the last of Robert Adam's life—he died in 1792—and show a trend towards a more elaborate and monumental style. The south side, now bereft of its decoration, bears a sombre air, but the east range with its great Venetian windows and delicate cornices, is a handsome composition. The houses are not large and have none of the elaborate finish of the Adelphi houses. The Duke of Grafton, it would seem, had families of moderate means in view as tenants and made no attempt to rival the social status of the Grosvenor and Portman estates.

Robert Adam's two ranges can have been only recently finished when the Duke of Bedford decided to carry out further development on his Bloomsbury property on the other side of Tottenham Court Road. His failure to prevent the building of the New Road may have finally decided him to demolish Bedford House and build several blocks of houses on the site. The work was in full swing in 1800, when Lady Holland wrote in her journal: "Bedford House is pulling down, and the Duke is building a new square." The greater part of the contents of the house were sold by auction, including Sir James

Thornhill's copies of Raphael's cartoons of similar size to the originals, which fetched rather less than £500.

The streets which grew on the site of Bedford House were the Duke's own enterprise, but a few years later the name which was to become synonymous with the building development of London, was first heard of in this district. Soon after 1820 Thomas Cubitt took a lease of a large area in the parish of St. Pancras from the Duke of Bedford and there laid out a network of squares and streets with names alluding to the Russell family or their country estates, Tavistock, Gordon, Endsleigh, Woburn, and so forth. Thus the whole of the large area of the original Southampton estate was finally converted from farmlands into bricks and mortar. The great works which Cubitt was soon after to carry out on the southern parts of Ebury Farm were to make his name even more widely known, but the ranges of stucco buildings in Belgravia were forestalled by John Nash's monumental terraces surrounding Regent's Park by a number of years. The former belonged essentially to the nineteenth century; the latter were the offspring of the eighteenth.

In the first half of the eighteenth century the village of Marylebone, which lay on the southern edge of a large rather wild area of Crown property, was still isolated from the tides of building creeping north and west from the metropolis. It still retained its rural air, which was enhanced by the sweep of open country to the north stretching away beyond the undulations of Primrose Hill to the steep and wooded heights of Hampstead. On the edge of this little village, so pastorally remote yet so convenient for the fashionable centres of the town, was laid out an agreeable public garden. "A place of public entertainment," it was described in *London and its Environs* of 1761, "which has a pleasant garden, and a band of vocal and instrumental music. This may be considered as a kind of humble imitation of Vauxhall." The gardens may have been humble, but they were exceeding pretty, with old trees and the Tybourne stream flowing through the grounds to the Marylebone basin, a sheet of water, like a broad canal, lying to the north of Cavendish Square.

In 1777 the gardens, after a fairly riotous existence of more than half a century, were closed and the area was let on lease with the fields which adjoined it on the north. Soon after the opening of the nineteenth century it was decided to develop this pastoral countryside in a new and special fashion. In developments in other parts of the metropolis, whether the Crown or a private person were the ground landlord, the plan had been very similar: a large square was set approximately in the middle of the estate and a grid of long streets, usually of rather economical proportions, were laid out round it. Any open space larger than a square was obviously not a financial proposition. The Crown, however, was able to adopt a less commercial plan: the great area of fields, covering nearly four hundred acres, was to be turned into a public park, in which full effect would be given to the stream so conveniently passing through it, while building would be confined to a circle of fine terraces bordering the park and a few isolated villas on the outer fringes.

In 1811 the lease of the Marylebone fields, which had been held by the Duke of Portland, expired, and in the following year the stupendous work of turning rough meadows into a public park and the raising of a series of great terraces of houses was begun under the supervision of John Nash. For a number of years the whole area presented an aspect of extreme chaos, levelling, cutting, excavating, building, the confusion caused by the making of the gardens at Versailles as portrayed by Hubert Robert was nothing compared to the pandemonium which reigned in the Regent's new park. In 1817 Hughson in his *Walks through London* remarks despairingly that it is "not likely to receive a speedy completion". His pessimism was amply justified, for it was not until twenty-one years later that the park was opened to the public. The laying out of Regent's Park was only a portion of a great scheme of urban planning which was materializing under Nash's direction. A splendid street, as wide and as majestically winding as a great river, was to lead from Carlton House in Pall Mall, cutting across a maze of narrow and haphazard streets to the northern extremities of the new park, where a spreading stucco palace was to be erected for the Prince. In the event the palace was not even begun and the Zoological Gardens now cover the site originally destined for royal gaieties; but Regent's Street was carried out approximately as contemplated except on almost the last lap where, owing to a disagreement with Sir James Langham, Nash was compelled to give his road an ungraceful twist in order to enter Portland Place. The whole conception was a fine one and the buildings which lined the street were attractive, though by no means great architecture; but at least the proportion of buildings to street was admirably adjusted to give an effect of space and light. Now, as the street winds between tall cliffs, the aspect is very different.

Regent Street was begun in 1813, and Nash here adopted the practice which Robert Adam had so successfully used in Adelphi Terrace and Fitzroy Square, of uniting long blocks of houses into a single composition. The design was simple but graceful, as befitted buildings designed primarily for commercial purposes, but in the terraces of houses round the park he adopted a more monumental and forceful manner. At the time of building and for many years after, the stucco surface which Nash gave to his buildings led to controversy: it would perish in the London air, it would flake off the walls, it would need constant painting. There were many arguments against it, but none, as it transpired during the following century, was entirely valid except the last, and this may be looked on rather as an advantage, since the terraces can recapture their original air of cheerfulness and cleanliness though admittedly at some expense. Portland stone on the other hand, though it weathers to a superb pearl grey, absorbs so freely the soot-laden air that deep black shadows are formed where none were intended by the architect and so disrupt the rhythm of the composition.

The terraces, all of which were given the names of peerages held by the Crown, show an infinite resourcefulness of variations on the same theme. But as a planner Nash was not the peer of Robert Adam, and in several of the terraces the amenities of the individual houses were sacrificed in some degree to the splendid and dramatic effect of the façades. Entrance halls are often dark and narrow, windows are not always placed to the best advantage in the rooms, and domestic convenience was not very carefully considered. But of the beauty of the exteriors there can be no two opinions; with their long Corinthian colonnades, low domes and majestic classical archways, each range has the air of a great country house rising from a setting of tall trees and spreading lawns. Nash's architecture has not always been appreciated: when his terraces finally rose and were freed from the confusion of the contractors' works they were greeted with a temperate enthusiasm, but by the middle of the nineteenth century they were already out of fashion, and were looked on as frigid, pompous and vulgar. Walford in his *Old and New London*, published about 1880, searched for a kind phrase. "These groups, undoubtedly, will not always bear the eye of a severe critic, but altogether they exhibit, perhaps, as much beauty as can easily be introduced into a collection of dwelling-houses of moderate size." Even this tepid praise must have been considered as excessive as similar remarks would now on the architecture of, for example, Pont Street or Elm Park Gardens.

It was not only the architecture of Nash which suffered from Victorian contempt: the several attractive villas which Decimus Burton built a few years later near the outer circle of the Park fell into equal disrepute within a quarter of a century or so of their completion. In 1855, when the contents of St. Dunstan's Villa, which Burton had built for Lord Hertford, were sold by auction, the house was disparagingly described: "the interior of this building is somewhat grotesque and irregular, it having been erected at enormous expense and by instalments, for the sole purpose of entertaining the Marquis's numerous friends." From the financial aspect the Regent's Park terraces were not a success. Though their appearance was at first admired, their situation was not considered convenient, particularly since a considerable area south of the park along the Marylebone highway remained as rough and undeveloped enclosures. Indeed, so slowly were the available houses taken up that for some time it seemed probable that the full scheme of building would have to be abandoned. However, there appears to have been just enough demand to warrant continuing, but it was not until about a century after the houses were built that the district became really residentially popular.

The experience which Nash gained in Regent's Park was of use to him in making his last and perhaps his greatest contribution to the architecture of London. The Prince Regent's sumptuous palace at Carlton House represented the work of a number of foremost architects. The principal transformation of an existing building had been effected by Henry Holland; James Wyatt, Nash and Thomas Hopper had further embellished the structure at huge cost to the public funds. In 1828 after a highly expensive existence of forty years, the house was demolished and Nash was commissioned to erect two terraces of large-scale houses on the site. The position was one of the finest in London. The prospect had not quite the romantic beauty of that over the river from Adelphi Terrace, but the view over the trees of the Mall and St. James's Park to the towers of Westminster could hardly be surpassed. As befitted the importance of the site and the size of the houses, the design of the two terraces was more forceful and much larger in scale than any of the terraces in Regent's Park, though the general design, with a long arcade of Corinthian pillars across the whole elevation, is not unreminiscent of the ranges of Sussex Place. The fortune of Carlton House Terrace is rather the reverse of that of Nash's northern buildings. For nearly a century the wealthy competed for the privilege of living in these magnificent houses, for to be an

York Terrace

Hanover Terrace

Sussex Place

NASH'S STUCCO COMPOSITIONS IN REGENT'S PARK

The Chelsea waterfront in 1744

Henry Holland's Pavilion and "Ruin" in Chelsea

Old Cheyne Walk, showing Queen's House

inhabitant of this exclusive terrace was to ensure a position in the social life of London. Now, however, its entrails are to be torn out in order to provide accommodation for the Foreign Office; while if the addition of substantial superstructures, which is at present contemplated, is carried out, it may well gravely injure the balance of Nash's dignified elevations.

The very moderate success of the Regent's Park scheme in no way discouraged speculative builders from raising houses for a similar class of tenant in other parts of London. Since the north-west area had proved a slow market, it was hoped that the south-west fringes of the town, which were far nearer the fashionable centres of the metropolis, would be more residentially attractive. The condition to the south and west of Hyde Park Corner was curious during the early years of the nineteenth century. Two highways led west and south; the former, the old road to Kensington and the west, skirted the long southern boundary of the park, and the latter followed the high wall of the great garden of Buckingham House, now fleetingly renamed St. George's Palace, where Nash was converting the old brick house into a dramatic and graceful building fit for the king. On the west side, the road was bordered by a line of seemly late-eighteenth-century houses, substantial and dignified in aspect though of no great architectural distinction.

Perhaps the greatest asset of these houses was their view across the road into the undulating garden of the palace. It was this eventuality which George III wished to avoid when he bought Buckingham House in 1762. At that time the garden was bounded by a minor road, while beyond it the open fields stretched away to the outskirts of Chelsea. The king obtained an option to purchase a long strip of land on the farther side of the road for the reasonable sum of £20,000, but Grenville, the Prime Minister, refused to sanction this purchase out of public funds, and the king was obliged to reconcile himself to the building of a row of houses just beyond his garden wall, the inhabitants of which would have a grandstand view of royal promenades along the garden paths. Between the two roads sweeping down the slope from Hyde Park Corner there remained, until a year or two after the death of George III an open space of rough marshy ground covering more than one hundred acres, which had formed the poorer pastures of Mary Davies' Ebury Farm. It was known as the Five Fields. Along the southern verge of the marshes a long straight road had been built in the last years of the eighteenth century leading to the farm buildings, on the site of now demolished Ebury Square, and on towards the fast-growing village of Chelsea.

Much had happened in Chelsea during the eighteenth century. Many of the large old houses, standing in their leafy gardens, had been demolished and rows of moderate sized, comfortable houses had been raised on the sites. They were houses built with little eye to architectural effect, their simple elevations evolving naturally from the sane planning of their interiors; but at that fortunate period, when good proportion in design and proper use of material and decoration came naturally to builders, architectural style seldom went amiss. Thus these reserved brick houses, with their panelled rooms and robustly designed staircases, have never, through all the passing vagaries of fashion, quite lost their residential popularity. When Thomas Carlyle came to London in the spring of 1834 he went to Chelsea in search of a small and inexpensive house. He considered himself fortunate to find one in Cheyne Row at a modest rent of £35 a year. It was a typical early Georgian house devised for those of moderate means, with two rooms on each story and little closets leading out of the back rooms on each of the two main floors. It suited Mr. and Mrs. Carlyle admirably, and here they remained until their deaths, hers in 1866 and his fifteen years later.

In 1858 Robert Tait painted a water-colour of the Carlyles in their drawing-room, which shows an interior very typical of that period. A wide doorway had been made between the front and back rooms and the double doors were clearly designed to be left open. A close-fitting carpet with a rather dominant pattern in red and deep blue covered the floor and joined the two rooms into a single unit. The walls were hung from dado to cornice with a flowered paper, and over the marble chimney-piece was a large square mirror in a gilt frame. A central table was shrouded in a patterned cloth, hanging in luxuriant folds to the floor, there were solid mahogany chairs with seats covered in black horsehair, and a sofa in a pink sprigged chintz. The general effect was perhaps a little teasing for present-day taste, but it was by no means ugly and gave an effect of warmth and adequate comfort.

Carlyle was not very critical of his surroundings, and came to the little house in Cheyne Row purely because the locality was agreeable and inexpensive. The same cannot be said of Rossetti, who after the death of his wife, Elizabeth Siddal, in 1862 left his house in Chatham Place at Blackfriars and came to live in Queen's House, in Cheyne Walk, the rent of which was £100 a year. The house was larger than he required, and rooms were let off to Swinburne and George Meredith, while Watts-Dunton sometimes spent a few nights in a rather uncomfortable attic. According to Rossetti's brother William, the house was "filled with Chinese tables and chairs, Dutch tiles, Flemish oriental and African curtains and draperies, looking-glasses and mirrors of the seventeenth and eighteenth centuries, a chandelier here and another there, and numerous knick-knacks of whatever kind". While the garden, which covered nearly an acre, was diversified with a small menagerie of animals: a kangaroo, a wombat and a racoon. The house, in fact, merely served as a convenient shell to contain a very catholic collection, and there was no attempt to suit the contents to the architecture.

Nevertheless early Georgian houses on the river bank seem to have had a special appeal for the Pre-Raphaelite brotherhood, for William Morris some years later moved into a large house of much the same date on the Upper Mall at Hammersmith. Rossetti was an early enthusiast for the art of Japan, the vogue about which W. E. Henley wrote: "It is more than a fashion, it is almost a craze . . . the Japanese dado has become almost a household word, and the Japanese fan a household essential." Morris's notions for making effective use of an early-eighteenth-century interior were even more curious than Rossetti's. His house contained a large drawing-room with five long windows overlooking the river, and into this classical shell he introduced the heavy oak furniture, the woven fabrics and highly coloured pottery which were the products of his various industries, "making the room a mass of subdued yet glowing colour", as J. M. Mackail wrote in his biography of Morris. No one apparently felt that anything was amiss; and indeed the objects in themselves had a merit which was rare at that deplorable period of taste, but they can hardly have appeared to advantage in that graceful panelled room intended as a background for gilded mirrors, gesso tables and Grinling Gibbons carving of an airy lightness.

Queen's House in Cheyne Row and those adjacent to it were built along the edge of the garden of the Manor House, which had been bought by Sir Hans Sloane in 1712 from William, Lord Cheyne. The garden was very extensive and a few years after his purchase Sir Hans decided to follow the prevailing fashion and develop the river frontage. This seemed a prudent measure, particularly as he was not living in the house, and did not in fact do so until thirty years after he had bought it. On his death Sir Hans bequeathed his Chelsea estate to his two daughters, the younger of whom was the wife of Lord Cadogan. Her heirs eventually inherited the greater part of the property. The gloomy marshlands of the Five Fields still formed a barricade between the metropolis and Chelsea village, but, though at this point London was not extending westward, Chelsea was slowly creeping eastward.

In 1771 Henry Holland was granted a lease of about eighty-nine acres by Lord Cadogan of his estate bordering the Five Fields, and building started almost immediately. Holland at this time was only twenty-six years of age, but already he had considerable architectural experience as assistant to Capability Brown, whose son-in-law he became in 1773. The necessary finance for the enterprise of laying out this area, which became known as Hans Town, was provided by Holland's father, who was a building contractor of eminence and wealth.

The long, rather narrow site did not lend itself to any very dramatic layout of streets and squares, and Holland contented himself at first with a single long, straight street leaving Knightsbridge at right angles and running undeviatingly southward towards Chelsea Hospital until it reached the boundary of the property. On the west of this thorough-fare, known as Sloane Street, Holland planned a fairly spacious square in the unusual form of an elongated octagon, into which streets entered at the two northern corners, while the south end was left open in order to provide a vista for his own house, which will be described in a moment. Hans Place, as the square was called, has now disinte-grated from an octagon into a figure of no particular geometrical shape. Within a decade a number of houses in street and place were completed and inhabited, and a few of these simple three-storied structures still survive; though particularly in Hans Place the majority were demolished during the later years of the nineteenth century to make way for buildings in the disastrously popular "Jacobean, Flemish" style. Hans Place was well established as a residential centre by 1802, when Letitia Landon, the youthful poetess whose fame did not long outlast her short life, was born there, and except for an interval of a few years, there lived until 1838, the years of her marriage and mysteri-ous death from poison. As a child she attended Miss Rowden's academy, which was only a few doors away from her home, a day-school where Miss Mitford and Lady Caroline Lamb had, a few years earlier, been an ill-assorted pair of fellow pupils. Jane Austen may well have seen the plump young Letitia, for in 1815 she came to stay in Hans Place in order to nurse her brother through a dangerous fever. The authoress of *Pride and Prejudice* was already famous, and her pre-sence in London became known to the Prince Regent. As a gracious gesture the Prince sent his librarian to call in Hans Place and invite Jane to visit the library and other apartments at Carlton House; he also added that he would be pleased to accept the dedication of Miss Austen's next book. Both invitations were rapturously accepted, and *Emma*, which was already in the press, was instantly given a loyal inscription.

Perhaps the most interesting part of Henry Holland's building enterprise was the house he erected for himself. Immediately to the south of Hans Place, on the present site of Cadogan Square and adjacent streets, he enclosed twenty-one acres of rough land and devised, with the aid of his father-in-law, a miniature estate laid out in the landscape manner. The house was designed about 1780, according to Dorothy Stroud's authoritative book on the works of this architect, and came to be known as the Pavilion, a name now commemorated by a long mews road, on the assumption that it served as a model for the house Holland was designing for the Prince Regent at Brighton. The owner, however, preferred the name Sloane Place, and in any case his house bore only small likeness to the marine villa, which was so quickly to disappear beneath Nash's exotic domes and pinnacles. The Hans Town building was simple in design, with a long colonnade supporting a balcony across the elevation to the garden. Though the scale was not large, the reception rooms, drawing-room, music room, library and dining-room were so arranged that communicating doors could be opened to make an enfilade a hundred and fourteen feet in length. A lawn lay before the house beyond which extended a sheet of water, so artfully planned and diversified by islands and promontories that it gave an appearance of great size. Statues and obelisks were set at suitable points amidst the shrubs which came to the water's edge, and to one side a romantic ruin, formed from stones brought from Cardinal Wolsey's great house at Esher, gave an agreeable air of antiquity and sweet melancholy to the surroundings. Holland died in 1806, but the house and garden survived for nearly seventy years longer, being inhabited by a number of distinguished tenants. Eventually the beautiful scene which Holland and Capability Brown had created disappeared to make room for urban development.

It was remarkable that while so much building activity was in progress on the eastern side of Chelsea that the great area of the Five Fields, owned principally by the Grosvenor estate and a smaller part, adjoining Holland's Sloane Street, by the Lowndes family, should have remained untouched by bricks and mortar. But the land was marshy and no speculator was inclined to take the heavy risk of converting the water-logged ground into suitable building land. About 1810 a few small streets had been protruded from the road bordering the Palace Garden, now Grosvenor Place, towards these gloomy quagmires, but they had stopped short on the edge of the lower lying area. In 1824, however, Thomas Cubitt fresh from his successful works on the Duke of Bedford's estate in Bloomsbury, boldly took a lease from the Grosvenor estate of a hundred and forty-four of these unpropitious acres. His task was formidable, but the proximity of the area to the fashionable parts of London and the *cachet* which had been lent to the whole district by the not distant presence of the royal palace promised a favourable chance of success. In addition Cubitt was not only a builder and contractor of great capabilities, but he was also a very acute business man.

Work was begun without delay, and a year after the lease was signed squares and roads were beginning to form a network over the derelict fields. The building estate was larger than any of those which had previously been developed as a single unit, with the exception of Regent's Park, which was planned on quite different lines, and there was, therefore, an occasion for creating vistas and perspectives which had not existed elsewhere. Up to a point the opportunity was seized: the principal square, named Belgrave after one of the landlord's minor titles, was planned on a noble scale covering an area of nearly ten acres, and the wide crescent, springing from its two northern corners is effective at least on plan, but there was no attempt to form a great vista from Hyde Park Corner to Sloane Street across the full length of the estate, which might have had great dramatic possibilities. Eaton Square was certainly laid out on long lines, but owing to the unforceful composition of the elevations it achieves monotony rather than grandeur.

Cubitt usually undertook the whole work of designing and building himself, since he had a grave distrust of professional architects. The great new square, however, clearly needed special treatment, and he overcame his scruples and invited George Basevi to undertake the design. Basevi, who was a first cousin of Disraeli, had worked under Soane, though he acquired little of his master's virile style. In Belgrave Square he made no attempt to emulate the elaborate terraces of Nash, but, probably under his employer's cold eye, designed simple but dignified compositions for each of the four ranges, with decoration severely controlled. On the frieze of the porch of the central house on the south side the author set his name "George Basevi, Architect, 1827".

In the past speculative builders had generally erected their houses and then awaited the appearance of prospective purchasers. The less fortunate were often still waiting when bankruptcy came to stare them in the face. This, however, was not Cubitt's method: he had a more prudent scheme, to which no doubt was partly due the vast fortune he left at his death. He constructed a single sample house, in Belgrave Square it is said to have been on the east side, and erected others only as commissions came in. Thus the square took many years to complete, the last house, that in the north-east corner, which was built for Sidney Herbert, not being completed until 1850. The detached corner houses, however, did not form part of Basevi's scheme, and in any case he had died five years before Sidney Herbert's house was finished, falling accidentally to his death from the western tower of Ely Cathedral, where he was supervising repairs.

In the interiors of the houses in the square, the architect was allowed little latitude: they, and indeed those of all the houses in the area, conformed to Cubitt's pattern of simple, well planned rooms possessing a minimum amount of dominant decoration. For, though the houses in Belgrave Square were built for individual tenants, Cubitt realized that London houses must be designed to please, and be adaptable to the taste of an ever-changing succession of inhabitants. The rooms, then, were designed to adopt whatever dress the occupiers cared to give them, and the fashions through which they have passed through their century and a quarter of existence are innumerable. The bland stucco façades have concealed, without losing a trace of their outward calm and dignity, interiors as various as one decorated by Lord Leighton to accommodate a collection of Pre-Raphaelite pictures, a dining-room riotous with the blue and silver detail of a German baroque palace, and, the present fate of all but a few, the light oak desks, typewriters and strip-lighting of government offices.

Until the large scale of the houses made them unsuited to the present restricted style of living, the square had maintained its position in the social world: though never quite reaching the fashionable peak of Grosvenor Square, its spacious, airy dignity made a constant appeal to those with sufficient wealth to live there. Some of the earliest tenants were royalty. In 1840 the Duchess of Kent, the mother of Queen Victoria, was living in the square, and three years later the Duchesse de Berri came here with her young son, the Comte de Chambord, in the hope of advancing his claim to the throne of France.

Oscar Wilde in 1887 placed the ducal home of Lord Arthur Savile in the square: the exquisite house where in the bathroom "the light stole softly from above, through thin slabs of transparent onyx, and the water in the marble tank glimmered like a moonstone". Thus residentially a high social pitch was maintained, but architecturally it passed through a period of considerable disapprobation during the dark middle years of Queen Victoria's reign, when the gloomy gothic style was so heavily in fashion. Augustus Hare voiced the popular opinion of Cubitt's stucco streets and squares when he wrote in 1877: "Belgrave Square is the only tolerable feature of this wearily ugly part of London." The change in taste was swift, for only a quarter of a century previously the spacious streets and brightly painted stucco of this new quarter had unexpectedly stirred the now forgotten poetess, Mrs. Gascoigne, to compose a long and spirited set of verses on the district. With enthusiastic and exclamatory pen she wrote:

> I sing Belgravia! that fair spot of ground
> Where all that worldlings covet most—is found!
> Of this stupendous town—this mighty heart,
> Of England's frame—the *Fashionable* part!
> Belgravia! favoured spot, that dost combine
> Beauties so far above all praise of mine!
> Thou of the gleaming walls and lordly crest,
> Oasis of the Fashionable West!

The extraordinary and rapid growth in the size of London during the century and three-quarters following the Restoration would suggest that the population had also increased with immense speed. But this was not entirely the case. In some measure the constant demand for houses of fair size was due to a change in the way of living. No longer were families prepared to be crowded together, as they had been when the City was the principal residential centre. Each family of consequence demanded its own house with plenty of space for entertaining, for accommodating a number of children and probably six or more servants. Louis Simond, whose *Travels in Great Britain* was published in 1815, was of the opinion that no family with less than £3,000 a year would think of migrating to any of the polite districts lying to the west of a line of longitude drawn through Soho Square, though he allows that the southern part of the meridian inclines to the east, and that it would have been rash to do so with less than £6,000. This would presuppose a great number of affluent families available to fill the elegant new houses, unless indeed there were many Becky Sharps

Regency Interiors

Carlton House, south front

The east wing of Carlton House Terrace

and Rawdon Crawleys able to give an air of prosperity when living precariously on their wits. At the time of the Great Fire there were computed to be 66,000 houses in London, and twenty years later the number had increased to 88,000, while the number of inhabitants had moved from half a million to 695,000. Sir William Petty, making his calculations during the latter years of Charles II's reign, computed that by 1802 the population of England would be 9,825,000 and of London 5,359,000. Remarkably enough, his estimate for all England proved to be little more than a hundred thousand above the numbers disclosed by the census, but his adumbration for the capital was quite incorrect as the population of London was only 900,000. This figure did not include such outlying districts as Chelsea and Kensington. Thus the inordinate expansion of London, which has been traced in the past pages, was carried out for the accommodation of only about 400,000 people, and though the metropolis had much more than doubled its size since the Restoration the increase in population had advanced at a slower tempo.

With building outstepping population, a much pleasanter way of life was brought about for those with sufficient means to buy or lease the new houses. No longer was there any necessity for several families to share a house, as had been very usual at a time when desperate official efforts were being made to control the expansion of London. During the eighteenth century the tendency had been the reverse, and in the leases of houses on the new estates there were often clauses forbidding the use of a house by more than one family. Miss Scott Thomson, during her researches amongst the Russell papers, discovered that as early as 1662 Lord Southampton included this proviso in the leases of some of the houses in his new square. Curiously, it was in the leases of the smaller houses and not the larger that this clause was found, and it must be presumed that the occupants of the latter would have been people of too high a position to consider sharing their dwellings.

More spacious living was not the only improvement: more hygienic living was also possible, since soon after the middle of the eighteenth century water-closets became more usual. As has been described, Robert Adam almost always included one of these invaluable features in his London houses, and they were gradually being installed in better-class houses built at a time when domestic drainage had been rudimentary. In Bedford House there were known to have been two in 1771, which may have been put in some years earlier, when both a hot bath and a cold bath were arranged. But it was many years before they became general. Writing of 1811 Louis Simond says, "rich houses have what are called water-closets;

The Cardinal. White The Deluge. Paper Box.
49/6 or 42/- 7/-
Ivory.

The Cardinal. The Deluge. Paper Box.
60/- 52/6 8/-

"Après Moi"

a cistern in the upper storey, filled with rainwater, communicates by a pipe and cock to a vessel of earthenware, which it constantly washes". He also compares very favourably the system of sewers in London with the lack of them in Paris, where "necessaries are emptied . . . poisoning the air of whole streets". A hindrance to domestic sanitation was the absence of a water supply to the top stories. To depend on rainwater was particularly unsatisfactory in a London house, where the roof area was small compared to the number of rooms it covered, though where water-closets were sited on upper floors this system was inevitable. In many smaller houses, and this prevailed until the nineteenth century was well advanced, the only convenience would be at the back of the house on ground floor or basement level.

Growing amenities were not all within doors: the condition of the streets was also fast improving, due to the ingenious inventions of two Scotsmen, William Murdock and John Macadam. Both, as it happened, were natives of Ayrshire and were born within two years of each

"Water-Closet for One Person"
(complete, ready for fitting up, £1 15s.)

other, in 1754 and 1756 respectively. The former was the inventor of coal-gas lighting, a discovery which has brought inestimable benefits to the domestic life of the nation. It was about 1800 when he first set up an apparatus for the making of gas in Messrs. Boulton & Watt's foundry

"One of the Advantages of Oil over Gas":
a topical cartoon by R. Dighton

in Soho, the firm by which he had been for many years employed as an engineer. In 1802 this capricious vapour, technically known as carburetted hydrogen, was used to add brilliance to the foundry's illuminations celebrating the peace of Amiens. Disappointingly enough, this first appearance of the discovery caused no sensation, indeed was only observed by a few. In the following year the invention was put to more practical purposes by using it to light the foundry; and this progressive example was soon followed by several other establishments. A few years later it was regarded with sufficient confidence for Mr. Ackerman to light his new library of the Arts by this means, and it was soon also installed in the remainder of his premises. But meanwhile Pall Mall had been fitted with an avenue of iron lanterns in which the fitful gas flames flickered and cast a modest brilliance on the long pavements. Inadequate though the light was, it was considered so great an advance on the former oil lamps that a company was incorporated, the Gas Light and Coke Company, to bring this amenity to all the important streets of the metropolis. The work did not apparently proceed with great speed, for Simond was not at all impressed by the lighting of Bond Street in 1811, which was still provided with oil lamps. "Little brightish dots," he called them, "indicative of light, but yielding in fact very little." Improvement, however, was at hand, and with it came added safety and convenience for those walking through the streets at night.

Macadam's system of road surfacing did not touch London until a few years later. By 1800 he had discovered, by constant experiment, that the most durable form of roadway was formed by putting down thin layers of small broken stone on a raised and cambered foundation; but it was not until after 1820 that the thoroughfares of London were treated in this way. The extraordinary improvement effected in the condition of the muddy or dusty streets of the metropolis was fully acknowledged, and Jeremy Bentham's tribute of 1825 in *Rationale of Reward* that "Macadam's system justified the perpetuation of Macadam's name in popular speech" voiced a general opinion. As it transpired the hope was fully accomplished.

As domestic comfort increased, so the standard of domestic architecture steadily declined. The grace of the eighteenth century persisted, with lessening strength, into the third decade of the following century, but thenceforward deterioration was rapid. Some not unattractive London houses were still to be built, but the sureness of touch which had existed in the past two centuries had disappeared: the innate feeling for proportion which had guided, like a guardian angel, simple builders to the creation of satisfactory works, was extinguished. From the opening of Queen Victoria's reign the designing of straightforward, pleasant-looking and convenient London houses became the exception instead of the rule, and it is rather the curious vagaries of taste which they exhibit than their architectural merits which provide an interest in the domestic architecture of this era.

V

Security and Comfort

With the death of the fourth of the Georges the spirit of the eighteenth century, which had survived under the leadership of this prodigal monarch, was finally extinguished. In no direction was this more apparent than in the field of domestic architecture, and was symbolized by the change from a king who had built Carlton House, the Brighton Pavilion and Buckingham Palace to one who preferred to live in a London house which was no larger, and was far more simply decorated, than the mansions of many of his richer subjects. The grand manner had not entirely died in 1830, but the grace, which was its essential accompaniment, had disappeared. Queen Victoria maintained or revived, after the seven-year lapse covered by her uncle's reign, the royal tradition of building by raising large houses at the two extremities of her kingdom, Balmoral in the north and Osborne in the south; but neither of these great structures had a trace of the elegance and distinction of George IV's palaces.

As with royal buildings, so it was with the domestic architecture of London. The tide of development never halted, indeed increased in volume, spreading its turgid waves round the already vast perimeter of the capital, but even in the politer and richer areas, which alone are here considered, the style and dash of the eighteenth century was lamentably wanting. Some pleasant enough little houses were built during the reign of William IV: the yellow brick and stucco of the Finchley Road, the closely united couples found in some of the streets of Maida Vale, all with a suggestion of *Cottages Ornés*, or the sober brick boxes with plain stucco shafts and deep cornices of Bloomfield Terrace at Victoria. There is enough to show that William's short reign produced a distinctive, if fleeting manner, a momentary respite before the deep plunge into the heavy and elaborate taste which prevailed during the remainder of the century.

There seemed to be no limit to the number of families which were climbing to prosperity and reaching a position in which they could afford a sizeable house, a staff of servants and a carriage. Thus the prospects for speculative building, particularly of houses for this class of family, remained exceedingly bright, and the only difficulty was to find suitable areas to develop which were not too remote from the centre of fashionable life. For a century this social fulcrum had been constantly moving, as has been shown in the earlier pages, but since the second half of the eighteenth century it had settled steadily in Mayfair. Thus it was within a reasonable distance of this desirable area that speculators in the early nineteenth century were constrained to search for fresh fields.

Immediately to the west of Mayfair the great wooded spaces of Hyde Park formed an insurmountable block between the metropolis and the growing village of Kensington, so that a junction between these two presented difficulties which had not existed between London and Chelsea. Highways, however, bordered the park on either side leading to the distant towns of Bath and Oxford; and that to the south, the Bath road, with a thin line of buildings along its southern verge, had formed a tenuous link of bricks and mortar between the metropolis and Kensington for many years. But to the north of the park the open country stretched away with no more than an occasional little village, farmstead or country house to break the pastoral landscape. In 1790 Paul Sandby painted one of his delicate water-colours of the Old Swan Inn at Bayswater. A winding lane leads past the timbered front of the inn, which seems to crouch beneath its thick covering of thatch, and up a gentle slope on which stand two timbered cottages; across the lane groups of tall trees rise above a long wooden paling within which, no doubt, was Hyde Park. No scene could be more intensely rural, and would seem to be laid in the leafy depths of some distant English county rather than within a mile or so of the fashionable centre of the capital. This arcadian prospect was by no means destined for immediate extinction when Sandby set up his easel opposite the Swan; indeed little major disturbance occurred for another forty years. Some development of a purely rural nature took place. It was found that this area, crossed by several streams of pure water and with a gravel soil, was suitable for the growing of watercress; and a number of beds were formed by the courses of the brooks. The industry thrived until the ground was required for more profitable purposes. Another agreeable feature of the district was the garden of the Toxophilite Society. It covered a space of four acres and was bounded by a stream, while an elegant pavilion to form shelter for members was erected on an eminence. There was space for six targets and a range of two hundred yards. The grounds were much frequented from the opening in 1821 until 1834, when, like the watercress beds, they were displaced by bricks and mortar.

Not far from the archery lawns stood Bayswater House, a house of no architectural importance, but to which a melancholy interest attaches since the last occupant was the forger Henry Fauntleroy. In 1807 Fauntleroy had become a partner in the banking firm of Marsh & Company, which had been founded by his father: seventeen years later it was discovered that he had embezzled sums amounting to £120,000 by forging powers of attorney over securities entrusted to his care. At his trial he explained that he had obtained these sums to bolster up the credit of his firm, which had been jeopardized owing to losses of over £100,000 in speculative building. It would have been interesting to know where these unsuccessful ventures took place and what was the cause of failure when so many others reaped a rich harvest. The unfortunate banker was found guilty and sentenced to be hanged, which, in spite of many attempts to obtain a reprieve, took place before a crowd estimated at a hundred thousand on 30th November, 1824. This was not quite the end of the story, for a persistent though apparently unfounded rumour arose after the execution that he had escaped death by the insertion of a silver tube into his throat which had prevented strangulation, and that having been restored to consciousness he had left the country.

Whatever the truth about Mr. Fauntleroy, there was no doubt that the existence of the Bayswater meadows in their pristine form was nearing its end. In the first years of Queen Victoria's reign "the splendid new town of Bayswater" was begun. The layout was traditional with squares, crescents and long streets, but the spirit of the eighteenth century was lacking. The long ranges of houses have, or had one should say since many have already been demolished, a bleak austerity, which Belgravia, of a little more than a decade earlier, had largely avoided. The tall stucco façades are for the most part designed without any softening embellishments, while the great height and clumsy proportions provide little pleasure to the eye. The exteriors are true mirrors of the interiors, which have high bleak rooms, suited, like the houses of Belgravia, to any schemes of decoration a succession of tenants may devise, but possessing a minimum of indigenous personality. The long straight road which runs between this dull but highly respectable district and Hyde Park was the rather unexpected site of the first experimental tramway laid in a London street. About 1860 an enterprising engineer with the appropriate name of George Train—a suitability perhaps only exceeded by Mr. Bell and the brothers Lumière, who invented respectively the telephone and the cinematograph—obtained permission to lay lines along this undeviating and gently undulating highway. The opening of the line was inaugurated with a great public banquet and the service was set going under the best auspices; but there was much opposition to this new form of transport, which was said to cause confusion amongst the existing horse traffic. It was many years before tramways were accepted as a useful, if noisy, feature of London streets.

Undoubtedly the builders of Bayswater achieved the objective for which they aimed. They had not hoped to oust Mayfair as the mecca of the *beau monde*, they had not even attempted to rival the Portman estate or Belgrave Square in residential style; but they had catered for the extensive and ever-growing class of middling prosperity. Many of the houses were large, but very few were vast, while the greater number were of a quite moderate size, according to lavish early Victorian standards. Thus Bayswater was inhabited, and for a century remained inhabited, by the class of people for whom it was devised. A very different fate befell the contemporary building estate, covering a great area lying between Belgravia and the river, known as Pimlico.

There is little interest to be found in this district beyond its name and its failure, at least from the social if not from the financial aspect. The origin of the strange un-English name remains as uncertainly fathomed as Piccadilly, and like the latter has been awarded a crowd of opposing derivations. An extinct race of Indians, a Hoxton innkeeper, a tropical bird, a textile material have all at times been put forward as the indubitable origin of the name, but not, it would seem, on any very sound foundation. It appears, however, that as early as 1630 the area now covered by the Stag Brewery in Buckingham Palace Road was known as Pimlico or Pimplico, and that from this site the name spread over the wide area of meadows stretching to the river. These pastures formed the southern section of Mary Davies' Manor of Ebury, and owing to their marshy nature, more water-logged even than the Five Fields, they appeared unpromisingly hazardous as potential building land. The experienced Mr. Cubitt, however, was not dismayed, and fresh from his great success with Belgravia, embarked with equal energy on the huge undertaking of laying out these wide swampy spaces as a polite and desirable residential locality. The general style was similar to Belgravia, but the scale was more meagre and economical, the houses smaller, the streets longer and more depressing. Monotony indeed was here brought to unusual heights: the long avenues of featureless stucco elevations, each punctuated by a plain pillared porch, are as dull and uniform as corridors of prison cells, and must always have seemed designed to crush all individuality. The streets were given high-sounding county names: Cambridge, Winchester, Cumberland, Warwick, and so forth; Lupus Street exceptionally striking a rather sinister note, until it is remembered that it commemorates the Norman founder of the Grosvenor family. With these amenities and the comparative convenience of the locality, it was surmised that the houses would appeal to those of moderate means and that the district would gain an air of respectable, if slightly threadbare, gentility. This rosy prospect was not, however, destined to materialize. Though a few of the squares maintained the intended standards, the greater part of the district sank swiftly and dejectedly down the social scale: the stucco peeled and mouldered, the plate glass of the sash windows lost its brilliance beneath a fog of grime, and washing suspended from upper windows indicated that houses had degenerated into tenements. Within a decade or two of their completion the once prim façades were concealing lives very different from those which the builders had optimistically expected.

Pimlico suffered social degredation to a degree which has never befallen the rival and contemporary area of South Kensington. The latter was more ambitiously conceived, with larger houses and wider streets, and it was confidently hoped that it might prove a formidable rival to Mayfair and Belgravia. If the movement westward, which had for so long been in constant progress, had been maintained, these expectations might have been fulfilled. But the South Kensington houses were built too late. The demand for big London houses began to diminish during the last decade of the nineteenth century. Slowly it became more difficult and more expensive to find servants to staff these mansions, six stories in height and of extreme domestic inconvenience. At the same time the invention of the motor-car led to a development of the habit of spending weekends in the country, and those not very rich preferred to have two medium-sized establishments rather than a single vast house in London. Those sufficiently wealthy to live on a grand scale both in town and country were inclined to disdain any district farther west than Belgravia. Thus many of the great houses of South Kensington, such as those in Cromwell Road or Queen's Gate, suffered a decade or more, from about 1895, of acute neglect, during which time these barrack-like houses, designed for large and prosperous families served by retinues of servants, stood empty, becoming yearly more unattractive to potential tenants. Eventually it was realized that their existence as single houses was

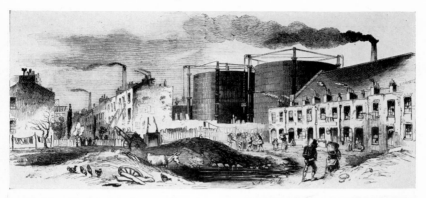

Some benefits of the age of gas

A corner of the Great Exhibition

Alma Tadema's Drawing-room in Regent's Park

THE VICTORIAN VOGUE FOR THE ORIENTAL

irremediably at an end and that their usefulness and financial productiveness could only be obtained in some new form. The solution was as hotels and flats, and as such these buildings have taken on a new life.

It was originally intended that Cromwell Road should serve as a great artery leading out of London, a gateway to the west lined with fine houses and museum buildings. However, as a gate it has remained for a century no more than ajar, and there seems little likelihood of it being widely opened in the near future.

It is difficult to envisage these gloomy and rather dilapidated streets and squares in the heyday of their prosperity, when opulence and comfort were to be seen on all sides. In the middle years of Queen Victoria's reign this condition was so unquestioningly accepted that this happy aspect was seldom described. An exception is in Hippolyte Taine's *Notes sur L'Angleterre*. The French historian spent the years of 1862 and 1863 in England, principally in London, and he viewed the town and country with the fresh, observant and critical eye of a young foreigner of thirty-four. He was particularly impressed by the fine houses to be seen in the areas round Hyde Park, those indeed which have been so disparagingly described in the past few pages, where every building was "Enduit d'un stuc blanc, luisant, vernissé; pas une tache de boue ni de poussière." All was in keeping: the well tended trees and velvet lawns of the square gardens, the brilliant flowers in the window boxes, the porches with two bells, one for visitors, one for tradesmen, the large windows, the basements for the servants, the stables relegated to a mews at the back, whence no smells would reach the politer part of the mansion. The French reaction to this spectacle of well ordered luxury was immediate: what income was enjoyed by the fortunate people who led these luxurious and spacious lives? It was exactly the same question which Louis Simond had asked half a century earlier. The latter concluded that at least £3,000 a year was required; Taine estimated a rather lower figure, and added: "Il y a dix de ces fortunes et de ces vies en Angleterre contre une en France."

Those who made fortunes in commerce, and there were many during the mid-Victorian years, gravitated naturally to these shining white houses in South Kensington or Bayswater. Only the very wealthy and the very bold amongst the *nouveaux riches* would dare to assault the exclusive purlieus of Mayfair, the Portman estate or even Belgravia. If they took the risk they often regretted it, unless their opulence was such that they could withstand a few aristocratic cold shoulders. Sir Gorgius Midas' preposterous sayings and ostentatious hospitality, which delighted the readers of *Punch* during the 'seventies and 'eighties, must undoubtedly have taken place in South Kensington. And Lady Midas' friends, Mrs. Ponsonby de Tompkyns and Mrs. Leo Hunter, seem certainly fixed for their arduous task of social climbing in this area.

The interiors which Du Maurier so brilliantly portrayed, with their heavy furniture, ponderous draperies, huge ornaments and dinner tables loaded, as Sir Gorgius assured his guests, with twenty thousand pounds' worth of plate, can have been no more than slight caricatures of the houses of rich *parvenus*, even if the figures moving in these opulent settings were rather exaggerated. But the successful merchant, the affluent sausage manufacturer like Sir Gorgius, and their families were beginning to penetrate with greater ease into social circles which would have been rigidly closed to them at an earlier period. Very great wealth seems always to have been a passport to admittance: Bubb Doddington, for example, in the early eighteenth century achieved the social eminence he wished for in spite of his lowly origin, and towards the end of the century the Portuguese Jew, Sampson Gideon, later Lord Eardley, entertained those considering themselves the cream of society at his pretty house of Belvedere near Erith in Kent, where there was an exquisite prospect over the breadth of the Thames valley to the gently undulating country beyond. Guests tittered at his pretensions, but did not hesitate to enjoy his hospitality. Indeed, both the rich through commerce and the practitioners of the arts were beginning to enter freely into fashionable drawing-rooms, and the titles bestowed by Prime Ministers on the former and by the Queen on the latter placed a comfortable seal on their social equality.

It was no longer possible to find large sites for single houses in the heart of London, sites which would allow of a spreading building surrounded by an extensive garden; but nevertheless vast houses were still being built. Stafford, now Lancaster House, which rose during the years following 1825, was rather exceptionally placed, on Crown property with the Green Park on one side and a fair-sized garden stretching to the Mall on another. Bridgewater House, a short way to the north, which was built from designs of Barry about 1849, was a gigantic building, but had no more than a modest area of lawn lying between its massive Italian façade and the park. Likewise the large detached houses in Belgrave Square, such as Seaford, were planned without even a few square yards of garden. The scale of all these houses would have pleased the great builders of the last Stuart and first Hanoverian reigns, but the inadequacy of their surroundings would have seemed to them miserable indeed.

All the houses just mentioned still stand, but the house which was in many respects the most interesting of the great nineteenth-century domestic buildings has vanished. This was Dorchester House, the existence of which extended to less than seventy years. The original house, standing between Park Lane and Deanery Street, was purchased by Mr. Holford in 1849; it was demolished and the massive new building, designed by Lewis Vulliamy, soon began to rise on the site, the elevations represented a rather severe rendering of the Italian Renaissance style, and soon, beneath the sooty London air, assumed a grim aspect, which was little livened by the golden gravel of the forecourt. But it was in the decoration of the interior that the interest lay, for here, amongst other artists, Alfred Stevens, probably the finest craftsman of the Victorian era, had carried out a number of embellishments. The house was planned with a huge central hall, through which a monumental staircase with balusters of English alabaster rose to a wide gallery, which surrounded the hall on three sides behind an arched colonnade. From the gallery opened the reception rooms, a great saloon, two drawing-rooms, a grand dining-room and a couple of sitting-rooms. It was decidedly in the grand manner. The Renaissance note was well maintained with damask-covered walls, windows set in frameworks of Corinthian columns and ceilings painted by Stevens, Anglinatti and Alfred Morgan.

Stevens' work in the house was still unfinished when he died in 1875 at the age of fifty-seven, but he had carried out sufficient, particularly in the dining-room, to show his abilities and his failings. The latter were exemplified in a majestic sideboard which he designed for a deep alcove at one end of the room. It was an elaborate structure of pillars, cornices and pediments, reflected in a backing of mirror; though carried out in wood, it was designed as if in marble, and was highly reminiscent of his Wellington Memorial in St. Paul's Cathedral. It was in fact more suitably adapted to support the ashes of the illustrious dead than for the modest and utilitarian purpose for which it was designed. Here, then, appeared his failing: his idiom was too grand for the simple matter he had to express. In the gigantic marble chimney-piece in the same room, however, he was at his best. The crouching figures supporting the deep, enriched frieze and cornice have a strength and grace which place them almost in the same circles as the works of Michelangelo.

Dorchester House, with its lavish decoration, was a prototype to some degree of the elaborate mansions built by the Vanderbilt family on Fifth Avenue in New York a few years later. William K.'s house was in the style of the early years of Louis XII's reign, when the Italian Renaissance had only lightly touched the architecture of France. Cornelius preferred the French château style of the seventeenth century, "with an harmonious interfusion of ideas adapted from the Flemish and Jacobean schools", as it was felicitously expressed. But the most ambitious was that of William H. Vanderbilt, the father of these two sons. It was built in brown freestone, in an indeterminate style with much carved decoration. The plan was rather similar to that of Dorchester House, with a large central hall surrounded by a gallery, but in this case the reception rooms were on the ground floor with bedrooms above. The decoration and embellishments of the large rooms were incredibly elaborate, showing a strong leaning towards the Italian Renaissance with velvets, marbles and much gilding of cornices, capitals and cherubs; while the greater part of the furniture, and the pictures which adorned the gallery, were of a style which is now almost worthless. There was undoubtedly a close union of taste between the two English-speaking countries.

In this country during the third quarter of the nineteenth century the rooms of the rich were dominated by the arts so lavishly displayed at the Great Exhibition of 1851. Standards of taste had been entirely transformed during the twenty years since the death of George IV. This monarch had passed away in an England still dominated by the taste of the Regency: there was an elegance and a simplicity in the design of both buildings and furniture, the prevailing appearance of rooms was still one of lightness, except in the homes of the devotees of the gloomier manner of the Gothic Revival; materials of curtains and on beds and furniture were generally light and delicate. By 1851, and the exhibits displayed were naturally in the forefront of public taste, the whole approach to furnishing and decoration had changed. Rooms must look sumptuous and rich, colours must be deep and glowing, velvets, brocades and reps had replaced the silks and muslins of twenty years before, while the grace and beauty of furniture would seem to have been determined by the amount of ornament and pattern which could be introduced without the least regard for what Inigo Jones called "decorum". It was fortunate that the invention of photography was at hand, so that representations of mid-Victorian rooms were faithfully recorded: without this truthful glass we might be inclined to doubt whether people could have happily framed their lives in surroundings of such elaboration and ugliness. Fine furniture,

A reception room in Dorchester House   Leighton's "Arab" hall in Kensington

The Grand Staircase, Dorchester House

Houses by Norman Shaw in Cadogan Square (1877)

surviving from a happier era, would be mingled without a qualm with objects of the meanest quality and value, and elaborate whatnots, sociables and basket chairs would oust from prominent places the finest works of Kent or Chippendale.

Not all the products to be seen at the Great Exhibition were hideous. There were Messrs. M'Cullum and Hodgson's tables, cabinets and workboxes made in papier mâché. The general form of these objects was certainly rather graceless, but the gleaming black surfaces, inlaid with mother-of-pearl and painted with scenes or flowers, were gay and pretty. The steel and brass firegrates, with their attendant accoutrement of fenders and fire-irons, were of the finest workmanship, but were set in marble chimney-pieces of unparalleled horror and elaboration. Some of the fabrics were very fine both in quality and in design, such as Messrs. Stone and Kemp's silks from Spitalfields, which were embroidered with exotic birds perched amongst bunches of luxuriant tropical leaves. But almost all the objects displayed, whether designed in good taste or more usually in bad, were pervaded by an air of ostentation amounting in many cases to vulgarity. Designers aimed at making their products look rich and expensive; this was the first aim, and in many cases, beneath the galaxy of machine-made ornament and finery, there was to be found very indifferent workmanship.

Surprisingly enough, there was one department of the Great Exhibition in which all the exhibits could be commended: all had grace, beauty and line. These miraculous exceptions to the prevailing heavy taste were the carriages. What could have been more exquisite than Messrs. Silk and Brown's "elegant park phaeton", with the sweeping lines of its body supported on swan-neck brackets and long curving springs? It is true that the decoration of the carriage was a little excessive, with the body in two shades of brilliant green and the wheels a pale primrose picked out with green and red, while the interior was "trimmed in a rich but chaste manner with green and white velvet lace". There were other phaetons, one for example designed like a nautilus shell, and a Canadian firm showed a sleigh in which the flowing lines were fully suggestive of smooth and effortless speed. These light and beautiful examples of coachbuilding were survivals from the taste of the early Regency: in this industry style had mercifully been retarded, and it was some years before broughams, victorias and landaus, which were so much better adapted to the way of life and outlook of the mid-nineteenth century, successfully ousted the phaetons and nautilus shells.

In general, however, the ponderous and elaborate exhibits set the fashion in furnishings for the following twenty years. The designs and styles which were so up-to-date in 1851 immediately appealed to public taste, and those who could afford these expensive objects, and they were many in those opulent years, hastened to discard such furniture as might have lingered on in their drawing-rooms from Regency or earlier dates and to replace it by exquisite objects such as they had lately viewed beneath Mr. Paxton's miraculous glass canopy in Hyde Park. The reception rooms of the new houses in Bayswater and South Kensington, so large and bleak as they left the hands of the contractors, were admirably suited to these majestic examples of the cabinet-maker's art, and to the large fluent canvases in—and this was essential—heavily moulded frames gleaming with gold leaf. Indeed the interiors depicted by Du Maurier can have only slightly exceeded the truth.

But this represented only the conventional taste, the taste of those with no taste, who had little or no personal feeling, but merely purchased the objects they saw in the shops. A more profitable and interesting study is provided by the houses of those with an inclination towards the arts, particularly those who were themselves successful artists. Substantial fortunes were made by painters who caught the public fancy, and a fine and prosperous-looking house was a part of their stock in trade. The more conventional of the residential districts of London were hardly suited to their purpose, and they usually set up their establishments in Chelsea, St. John's Wood or the leafy purlieus of Holland Park. It was in the last of these that the only English artist who has ever been rewarded with a peerage, Lord Leighton, decided to build his house.

From the first Leighton had been extremely successful, and his vast canvases, usually representing buxom nudes in a mythological guise, commanded immense prices. The house, therefore, which George Aitchison erected for him about 1866 was designed to be a mirror of his achievements. The massive red-brick exterior was a breakaway from the prevailing style of stucco building, though, beyond the material it showed little initiative; but the oriental manner of the interior was—and is, for the house still stands—highly symptomatic of the more sensitive impulses of the age. There seems now little beauty in it: the Moorish arches, the ebonized woodwork of the staircase with bulbous balusters, and the great areas of viridescent tiling are no longer sympathetic; and we should have appreciated it little more if we had seen it with its full furnishings of brass pots, oriental jars and stuffed peacocks. Similarly the Arab Hall, which faithfully reproduces detail found in buildings in Moorish Spain, seems now no more than dark and mournful exile from the heat and brilliance of the country which gave it origin. It is difficult to comprehend the ecstasies of contemporary writers, who were enthusiastic about the "enchantment", the "coolness" and "the oriental repose" of these rooms. These are perhaps qualities of which we have lost the value. There was, however, one feature of the furnishing of the house which would have had the full approval of modern taste: this was the collection of pictures, excepting, it is perhaps needless to add, the owner's own works. On the walls were to be seen many examples of the paintings of the Barbizon School, landscapes by Corot and Daubigny; in addition, and even more to the taste of today, there were a great number of first-class works by Constable, including a sketch for the *Hay Wain*. There were also a Tintoretto and pictures by Reynolds, Delacroix and some Italian masters. After Lord Leighton's death in 1896 these pictures were sold for prices far in excess of those he had originally given: an indication that in some directions at least the famous artist's taste was ahead of his time.

Aitchison's services were constantly in demand for the redecoration of houses. A handsome commission was to give a contemporary flavour to one of the late Stuart houses in Berkeley Square. A full description survives of the drawing-room he contrived within this sober dignified fabric and may well be quoted:

"The doors have frames of ebonized wood, enclosing panels of finest grained amboyna. The ebonized wood is foliated with gold and the low central panels are adorned with ovals of olive-coloured Wedgwood ware, representing classical figures. Each door has a capping of gold floriation and a draping of French embroidered silk at once heavy and delicate, like tapestry. The walls are of a dark reddish-brown colour enclosed in large panels, outlined by a fine painted edging. The ornament which chiefly strikes the eye is a matchless frieze, painted by the eminent artist Albert Moore, the design being peacocks, their long trains in repose. The cornice above this is of the egg-pattern, with a fretting above. The ceiling is in a manner panelled, with crossbeams finely feathered with gold."

There was much more in this style such as an elaborate chimney-piece, brilliant tiles on the hearth and an ingenious grate which could be pushed in and out according to the amount of heat required.

There were, of course, a number of large Japanese screens. The room must have presented an appearance of remarkable ugliness and vulgarity, and yet it was not the conventional taste which was founded on the Exhibition. The influence of William Morris and his colleagues can be detected in the colour of the walls in the peacocks and in the beamed ceiling.

In the elaborate house in St. John's Wood of Alma Tadema, the painter of jejune but extremely remunerative pictures, the same feeling was found beneath a cosmopolitan galaxy of styles. The library was predominantly Gothic in spirit, with furniture also in this manner, including perhaps some of the monumental pieces designed by Pugin and made by Crace, which crowded the Medieval Court at the Exhibition. The drawing-rooms in contrast were predominantly oriental in aspect, with Persian velvets on the walls, thick oriental carpets on the inlaid floors, and chairs and sofas heaped with cushions. The windows were glazed with Mexican onyx, which suffused the rooms with a dim amber light. The Gold Room was even more gorgeous: the entrance was draped with a Chinese silk curtain in yellow, blue and gold, the floor was of ebony and maple wood, round the walls was a Byzantine dado five feet in height surmounted by a miniature copy of the Parthenon frieze carved in ivory and set in an ebony frame. As a background, every vacant space on walls and ceiling was covered with gold leaf, and here also the windows were of onyx in a lead setting, so contrived as to form the initials of the owner and his wife. This sumptuous decoration far exceeded the rugged principles of Morris, but amends were made on the staircase, where Morris's own pomegranate paper covered the walls above a dado of brown-coloured matting: this had the true flavour of the Red House at Bexley or of Kelmscott Manor.

Rossetti's interest in the art of China and Japan and the oriental air he gave to his house in Cheyne Walk have already been mentioned. A little farther along the river bank, in a section of Lindsay House, Whistler was also decorating his home in the same manner. His drawing-room was lined with fifteen large Japanese panels representing flowers, foliage and birds painted in brilliant colours, while Japanese fans and Chinese plates and cabinets of the same *provenence* played a part in the decoration. It was not only in England that the art of Japan was in such high favour during the eighteen-seventies: simultaneously in Paris Edmond de Goncourt and his friends were collecting prints and porcelain with almost hysterical enthusiasm.

A now little remembered figure, but one who in his day was considered by many the foremost decorator in England, is Owen Jones. He came to the fore with the Great Exhibition, where he designed a number of the interior embellishments, and added to these when the Crystal Palace was removed to Sydenham. The Prince Consort was much impressed by his accomplishments, and the Shah of Persia wished to take back to his country Jones's reproduction of the Alhambra Rooms. It seems to have been principally his work which led the writers of the official catalogue of the French Exposition of 1867 to acclaim England as "the leader in decorative art". He died in 1874 and passed quickly into oblivion.

Fortunately a description exists of a very lavish interior he created some years before his death for a rich industrialist, Mr. Alfred Morrison. The house was in Carlton House Terrace, and the writer lamented the ugliness of Nash's classical range. "It repeats," he wrote, "the apparent determination of ages that there shall be no external architectural beauty in London." What a happy chance, then, that Mr. Jones was at hand to bring beauty, comfort and convenience to the interior. It was a very large house, and from every room of importance all evidence of its Regency origin was carefully removed: the stage was then ready for the introduction of woodwork made from an infinite variety of English and foreign timbers. "In the dado, jambs, chairboarding, we find no carved work, but simply the most exquisite combinations of ebonized and many coloured woods." In the library there was an early presage of *art nouveau* in the doors of the bookcases, which were "adorned with a foliation, over two feet high, growing from the bottom of the panel and leafing out at the top". Some of the rooms were lined with silk specially made at Lyons and designed by Jones, who also provided drawings for the carpets woven in Persian style. The drawing-room we learn was adorned with a fretted ceiling, a frieze of damask picked out with gold, a tarsia dado, and marble chimney-pieces, which Lepec of Paris had spent two years in carving. Against this background were set Buhl cabinets, an iron coffer, on which a Spanish workman had laboured for over four years and been paid over a thousand pounds by Mr. Morrison, there were also chairs "nearly every one of which was different from the other—one suggesting the perforated chairs of the Delhi palaces, and another the old Saxon throne in Westminster Abbey". It is not quite clear whether Owen Jones was attempting to reproduce a "period" interior or whether he was aiming at creating a unity entirely of his own creation. If the former was his objective it is difficult to say at which point in history he was directing his invention, though the later years of the French Renaissance would seem to be a hot favourite.

In Owen Jones' decoration the *art nouveau* note was very lightly, almost insensibly, introduced; but in a few other houses more definite examples were to be found. In one of Aitchison's houses the entrance hall was lined with green panelling which was ornamented with "stems starting from a common root and ending each in cones. The stems and cones curve towards each other, and form a sort of circular grouping". Here appears the true note of this transient style, that endeavoured to produce the impression of sub-aqueous plants twisting upwards in gentle undulations through dim, deep water to a distant surface. This theme was introduced with little regard for its suitability into the design of simple pieces of furniture, chairs, tables, beds and wardrobes, all of which would be endowed with a rather alarming sense of rhythm: while in decoration these sinuous stems would wind round doorways and over chimney-pieces. In the medium of bronze alone it seems to achieve a genuine grace and beauty, as can be seen for example in some of the works of Alfred Gilbert, such as the Queen Alexandra Memorial Fountain, which represents perhaps the last manifestation of this style. But on the whole there was little to be seen in London, and it is in France, where it flourished during the last decade of the century, that the finest examples are to be found. In the Musée des Arts Décoratifs in Paris is preserved a room removed from a private house in which tall trees, carved in oak in semi-relief mount from floor to ceiling encircling in their branches sheets of mirror and large canvases portraying pastoral scenes. Nothing of a similar nature was ever produced in this country; nor fortunately did we emulate the fashion as it blossomed in Spain, under the direction of Señor Gaudi, into the neo-Catalan style. In Barcelona Gaudi created a nightmare district, like a setting for some of the more sinister of Grimms' fairy tales. Tall concrete trees and plants writhe upwards on the façades of the houses, while windows, formed in all manner of strange shapes, peep out amongst the petrified trunks and branches, and patches of bright mosaics lend a little garish colour to the design. His most ambitious building was the Templo de la Sagrada Familia, a circular cathedral; but barely half the structure was completed when in 1925 the aged architect was killed by a tram, and work was stopped. Now this strange shell is gradually mouldering into decay.

Although *art nouveau* played so little part in the average English house, its faint spirit was indicative of and contemporary with a new feeling which was growing in domestic architecture. As has been seen, the classical terraces of Nash were already considered ugly within half a century of their completion. This revulsion from cold grandeur and rigid uniformity was in a large measure due to the works of William Morris and his friends. They advocated a robust individualism and a return to the arts and crafts of medieval England. In this ideology graceful ranges of stuccoed houses or Adam's elegant classical composi-tions had no place at all. The building of the Red House represented the first step in the new direction. It was designed in 1859 by Philip Webb for William Morris, and incorporates, both in its structure and in its interior decoration and fittings, the intransigent principles for which the Pre-Raphaelite brotherhood stood. Though it was a house standing in the open country, it was to be the forerunner, as regards general style and intention, of a great number of houses subsequently built in the new residential areas and in the suburbs of London. It was not, however, by Webb that the flood of red brick was guided over so much of the metropolis, but by Norman Shaw, a shrewd Scotsman, whose architectural practice became one of the largest of his time.

Undoubtedly a change in the style of London Houses was overdue. The manner which Nash had introduced with such brilliance had degenerated into the almost insupportable monotony of the duller South Kensington streets. The style had been done to death: there was no longer hope of infusing any life or beauty into this moribund body. Thus the last flicker of eighteenth-century tradition was finally extinguished a decade or so after the middle of the following century; and there can now be few regrets, for like a grand personality in decay, it presented a spectacle which could only sadden, while the new style, crude and immature in many directions, had at least the merit of liveliness and fresh ideas. The whole attitude was different. The eighteenth-century builders of streets and squares had approached their problems in an entirely logical manner: their houses were frankly one of an urban row and were carefully designed as such. In this way great success was achieved. Norman Shaw and some of his followers had other aims: they tried to give their urban buildings a country air, often the air of a manor-house built during the reign of William and Mary, when the Dutch influence was strong, which had been engulfed by later building. This aim was successfully reached by Norman Shaw on occasions, such as in the fine but grim building of New Scotland

Yard, or the more welcoming block of flats at 1 St. James's Street, but the few houses he built in Cadogan Square in 1877, with their narrow frontages, have the air of being squeezed uncomfortably upwards by their ponderous neighbours or of being reflected in a distorting mirror. In central London it was obviously difficult to bring about the effect desired, but in the outskirts of the town Shaw was presented with some first-class opportunities, and nowhere better than in the new quarter of Bedford Park.

In the countryside a number of model villages had been built since the last decades of the eighteenth century, but Bedford Park represents the first attempt at a form of urban building which subsequently became popular as a garden city. The colonies at Hampstead and at Welwyn, at Port Sunlight and Bournville, are the direct descendants of Norman Shaw's innovation. The district lay to the north of the Chiswick Road, and until well past the middle of the nineteenth century had been covered with orchards and meadows, in the midst of which stood Bedford House, the home of the famous botanist and horticulturalist John Lindley, who planted his garden and surrounding grounds with many rare trees and shrubs. Dr. Lindley died in 1865 and the property, covering a hundred acres, was sold to a Mr. Jonathan Carr, who conceived the idea of forming here an intellectual colony, principally of those interested in the arts. He planned so to lay out the roads and set the houses that the majority of the fine trees could remain. The intention was that this new suburb should have the haphazard air of an old country village. Mr. Carr enlisted the professional assistance of Norman Shaw, and the scene which they together created was far from unsuccessful. Within five years about three hundred and fifty houses had been built, with a number of shops, and even a public house, the Tabard Inn, conceived on rather genteel lines. Brick and tile were the predominant materials, and the architectural style varied a little uncertainly between the vernacular and that of Queen Anne's reign; Shaw made considerable play with his favourite features of tall brick chimney-stacks and overhanging gables. The houses were usually designed singly or in pairs, terraces were eschewed, except in the shopping centre, where there was a range of buildings of some length.

The finest house was Mr. Carr's own, the Tower House, which in style was rather reminiscent in design of Eagle House at Mitcham, itself a modest rendering of Sir Roger Pratt's Coleshill. The brick walls were topped by a deep wooden cornice from which the roof rose steeply to a central flat surrounded by a balustrade. In the centre of the flat was set a tall cupola. However, the bow windows and large dormers lent an unmistakably nineteenth-century air to the building. The interior struck a more Jacobean note, with heavy wainscoting covering uncomfortably a little more than half the height of the walls and Morris papers filling the space to the heavy cornices. Elaborately carved overmantels and massive furniture designed in the same rather unhappy style completed a ponderous scene, and one rather blatantly conscious of good workmanship. This indeed was the quality above all others at which those concerned were aiming, and it was described very accurately in the *Sporting and Dramatic News* in 1879: "There is no attempt to conceal with false fronts, or stucco ornament, or unmeaning balustrades, that which is full of comfortable suggestiveness in a climate like our own—the house roof; everything is simple honest and unpretending."

An amenity which Mr. Carr provided, and which would have seemed singularly out of place in any of the eighteenth-century building estates, was a social club. There was a large assembly hall, a reading-room lined with seventeenth-century panelling and lighted by a long flight of lattice windows set in wooden mullions, and a billiard room. A difficulty arose over the latter room, one of the few clouds which apparently ever darkened this successful and fraternal enterprise. It arose from the fact that the ladies of the colony wished also to play billiards but thought it indelicate to enter the room, since the men often smoked there and occasionally removed their coats. The benevolent and perspicacious Mr. Carr quickly settled the trouble by building a second billiard room, where energetic women could indulge without embarrassment in the game, so far as the close-fitting tunics and voluminous skirts of contemporary fashions would allow.

At Bedford Park Norman Shaw was able to give full expression to his semi-urban style: in other parts of London he was more restricted. But on the spacious Hampstead slopes, where building was just beginning to join this hill town to the swelling metropolis in the valley, he could indulge his feeling for romantic grouping with comparative freedom. The large house he built for Edwin Long, an extremely successful artist of the mid-Victorian period, but now utterly forgotten, was an example of the spreading style and planning which he favoured when opportunity arose. The house did not long survive and there is now no record of how the great corridor, spacious staircase and huge studio were furnished: did Edwin Long emulate Rossetti's catholic collection, Leighton's oriental splendour, or Alma Tadema's cosmopolitan display? There is now no indication, but it is probable that his fancy lay towards the east, since the highly remunerative scenes which he liked to portray were generally given an exuberant Moorish setting.

"A Town House Dining-Room" designed by
R. Norman Shaw, R.A.

Long's house was in Netherhall Gardens; close by in Ellerdale Road, Shaw built another house with an interior entirely after his own heart, for it was designed for his own occupation. Now, graced with the name Hampstead Towers, it stands closely hemmed in by later neighbours. The dining-room was a particularly good example of his early style. It was a high room lighted by long lead-paned windows and with a heavily beamed ceiling. The greater part of one side of the room was taken up by a gigantic inglenook, which was so contrived that a narrow stair at the side led up to a little chamber, a perfectly useless room, above the ingle with an elaborate lattice window, set in a surround of Italian Renaissance style, opening into the upper air of the dining-room. The face of this chamber to the dining-room was decorated with enriched bands of plaster, between which were strips of lincrusta. A large area of tiles round the hearth, a number of oriental and majolica plates and vases, a brass chandelier and the decorative elements of the room were complete. From the standpoint of the present day the effect achieved was dull and gloomy and singularly unsuited to London, where daylight can ill be spared, but there was a competence in design and a scholarly use of detail and decoration that made it at once clear that this was a room created by a man skilled in his work.

Norman Shaw's services were much in demand in many parts of London. On a fine open site in Kensington Gore he built Lowther Lodge which was completed in 1873, a year after Sir Giles Gilbert Scott's Albert Memorial had risen before the dazzled eyes of Londoners close by on the verge of Hyde Park. The Lodge, shorn of all but a small area of its garden, now shelters the Royal Geographical Society. It is a typical example of Shaw's romantic manner, with towering chimney-stacks, tall windows and moulded brickwork in Renaissance style. The same theme, with an even more pronounced Dutch feeling, was introduced in the elevations of the houses already mentioned in Cadogan Square, which were built four or five years later. The planning of these tall houses was a complete breakaway from the conventions of the eighteenth century or those favoured by Cubitt. The simple arrangement of rooms found in the moderate-sized houses of Belgravia, a long hall leading to a staircase, with two rooms at the side, a large in front and a smaller at the back reduced to allow space for the stair, was beginning to pall as the third quarter of the nineteenth century opened.

A writer in *The Magazine of Art* voiced a very general sentiment when he wrote: "The average 'front and back' houses, say of the type found in Eaton Place, is about as meanly arranged as a house can be." Architects, many less capable than Norman Shaw, rushed eagerly in with new ideas for giving interest and an air of space to their new

9*

houses. It was very rarely indeed that their complicated and tortured plans showed any improvement on the simple arrangement devised by their predecessors. Norman Shaw's planning in the Cadogan Square houses certainly exhibits ingenuity, but the houses must always have been gloomy and devoid of daylight. The two principal features at which he aimed, and to which all else seems to have been sacrificed, were a large entrance hall and an enormous drawing-room. To achieve these ends he placed the hall across the whole frontage of the house, formed an *entresol* above for a dining-room and library, and placed a drawing-room extending from front to back of the house above these two rooms. The long flights of the staircase mounted gloomily in the heart of the house, lighted fitfully by a little borrowed light glimmering dimly through coloured glass of Morris-like design and from a skylight far above at roof level.

Now that these houses have been put to other than domestic uses it is difficult to assess how effective their original decoration can have been. In all the principal rooms there is plenty of woodwork, panelling and wainscotes, heavy wooden cornices, elaborate, rather Jacobean effects surrounding inglenooks, which latter are conceived on a majestic scale, and several rooms have dark, beamed ceilings. The leaded lights of the windows, which are not ineffective from outside, obscure all but the rays of the brightest sunshine, so that the rooms are dark except on the most brilliant days. It must be generally agreed that Norman Shaw, in spite of his elaborate planning, had achieved no improvement at all on the "meanly arranged" houses of Belgravia.

These houses were amongst the first constructed in the large new square laid out on the site of Henry Holland's Pavilion and its romantic garden, and had the whole square followed in a similar manner it would have at least been a remarkable monument to a highly skilled architect. But in the event the remainder of the square, in company with many of the neighbouring streets, were built up with houses of little interest or distinction; and the dark brick and terra-cotta decorations which prevail all over this district seem to us as gloomy now as the stucco of Belgravia did to Augustus Hare just over seventy years ago.

Style in architecture and taste in internal decoration are never stationary, and the London homes described in the past pages were to undergo constant alteration through the ever-changing gamut of fashion. Good and bad taste advanced hand in hand through the last years of the Victorian era and through the brilliant, ostentatious reign of Edward VII, and so, over the shattering hazards of two world wars, to our own bleak times. The bad taste displayed during the two decades on either side of 1900 seems to us now very bad, the good taste not very good; and one wonders how the decorative arts of these middle years of the twentieth century will strike those living when the next century opens. The zest and gusto, and one may add the wealth, which gave such liveliness to earlier periods have now largely vanished, and the rather careful taste of today is either retrospective or uncertainly advanced. It is unlikely that in half a century's time this will be looked on as a great creative age.

In the residential heart of London no areas now remain to be built up: the layout covering Henry Holland's garden represented the last of the long sequence of developments which gave the central area of the metropolis its present aspect. Such grim thoroughfares as Victoria Street in Westminster and Queen Victoria Street leading to the City were forged through mazes of small streets in imitation of Baron Hausemann's boulevards in Paris, but there was nothing residential about these new highways.

Construction in steel and concrete has brought great changes to the aspect of the streets, and many attractive houses have been demolished to make way for these more economic structures. As a result the London home, which was for centuries perpendicular, is now fast becoming predominantly horizontal; and the individual town house, the single feature perhaps which the great towns of the Continent have consistently envied in our rambling old capital, seems destined soon to take its final curtain.

Index

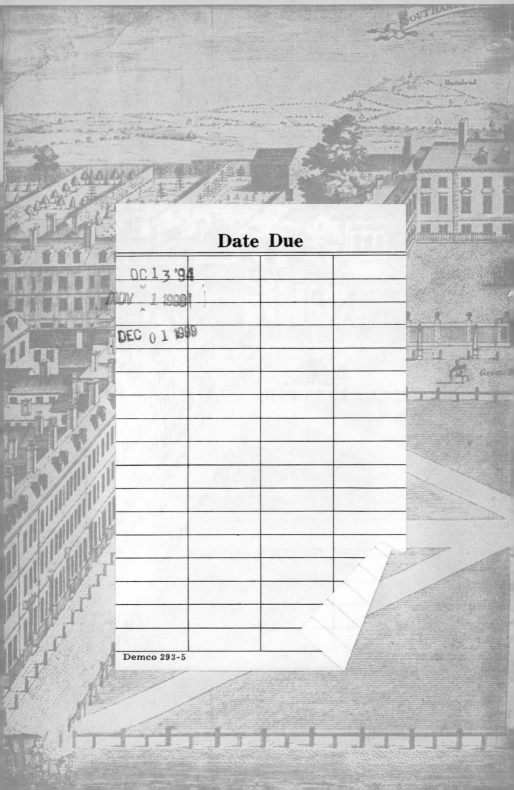

Date Due

OC 13 '94		
NOV 1 1998		
DEC 0 1 1999		